Live Well

Live Well

The Letters of
Sigrid Gjeldaker Lillehaugen

EDITED BY

Theresse Nelson Lundby
Kristie Nelson-Neuhaus
Ann Nordland Wallace

WESTERN HOME BOOKS
MINNEAPOLIS

Most Western Home Books are available at special quantity discounts for bulk purchases for sales promotions, premiums, fundraising, and educational needs. For details, write

Western Home Books
Syren Book Company
Special Sales Department
5120 Cedar Lake Road
Minneapolis, Minnesota 55416

Published by
Western Home Books
An Imprint of Syren Book Company
5120 Cedar Lake Road
Minneapolis, Minnesota 55416

Printed in the United States of America on acid-free paper

ISBN-13: 978-0-929636-30-6
ISBN-10: 0-929636-30-9

LCCN 2004106508

To order additional copies of this book see the order form at the back of this book or go to www.itascabooks.com

Contents

Foreword

During my trip to Hallingdal, Norway in 1992, I was privileged to visit the archives to see firsthand the artifacts and letters in the Gudmundsrud files. Ola Hagen of Ål, Hallingdal, whom I had met at meetings of the Hallinglag of America, arranged the visit. While there, I arranged to receive copies of letters written by Sigrid Gjeldaker Lillehaugen to her father, Lars Gjeldaker, during the years 1892 to 1923. It appears that a few letters may not have been preserved, but we are grateful for the letters that were protected by the family and donated to the archives.

I would like to thank Ola Hagen, who generously shared genealogical information of the Norwegian Hallings. I am indebted to Gladys Jorgenson Peiler, who translated the letters

Theresse Lundby, Ola Hagen, Olga Berglund in Norway, September 22, 1992

from Norwegian into English. I am also indebted to Shirley Lillehaugen Santoro for her continued interest in the project; to Ann Nordland Wallace and Glenn Wallace, who transcribed the letters; to Kristie Nelson-Neuhaus, for her expertise in editing, managing the project, and arranging for the printing of this book; and to Paul Neuhaus, who handled all graphics, photos, and designed the cover. A sincere thank you to each one!

My hope is that this book will be treasured by family members and will be of interest to others who enjoy early day history.

Theresse Nelson Lundby

Introduction

In 1885 Sigrid Gjeldaker Lillehaugen emigrated from Hallingdal, Norway to America with her three children, Anna, Micheal, and Lars. She joined her husband Tosten in Minnesota, and in 1888 they homesteaded in Dakota Territory.

The letters in this book start in 1892. Sigrid wrote first to her father, Lars Gjeldaker, and later to her stepmother, Birgit Myking Gjeldaker.

Sigrid vividly describes pioneer life and its seasonal rhythms. She also sends news and greetings from her neighbors, many of whom her family knew well from Hallingdal.

But most of all, Sigrid writes about her children. Her father knew the oldest three, the next eight were born in America. Letters and pictures were her only means of conveying the story of her children—their experiences, personalities, talents, and accomplishments.

Sigrid was from an educated family in Norway; both her father and grandfather were renowned teachers. Throughout her letters Sigrid describes her children's education, reassuring both herself and her father that even though they lived far away in America, her children were intelligent and excelling in their studies.

In Sigrid's early accounts, life is full of activity—buying land, building homes and barns, having children, welcoming new emigrants like her brother, Knut. In the middle years, the older children marry and start their own families, while younger ones attend school far away. There is also sorrow. Sigrid recounts the deaths of five of her children, Amanda, Lars, Nels, Theodore, and

Clara. In the final letters, only Sigrid and Tosten remain at home, and Sigrid reflects on life and aging.

While preparing this book, we have tried to remain as faithful as possible to Sigrid's original letters, making only minimal edits for consistency. We have also included an annotated list of letters, family trees, historical notes, time lines, and additional information about the Gudmundsrud family.

Live well,
Kristie Nelson-Neuhaus

List of Letters

Live Well

Lillehaugen
February 25, 1892

Dear unforgettable Father! Mother and Brothers,

Now that at last your long-awaited letter has come, I want to send you my thanks for the letter. I often wondered why Father waited so long before he sent us a letter. How lovingly welcome to receive your dear familiar hand again and read the dear lines from Father. Yes, I thank God for letting that happen. With gladness I see that everything is well with you at home. And the same I can say from here because we have our health to date, which is the best of everything good. God gives us His grace.

First we must tell you that on November 4 we were blessed with a little well-shaped son, Theodore, who now is growing and bright for his age.

The crops were good last year, the first wheat harvest in Dakota. Now we will see if it will be better here. Some have given up their land and moved away.

Tosten and Micheal have much work in the barn, as we have many animals. They also bought a team of horses. There is much to buy when a man is beginning to farm, and here it is expensive. Machine and tools we need, but we are afraid to buy before we can pay.

You have now met with Knud Jallo from here who is in Norway, and then you can hear how it is with us. We have had much snow this winter, almost like Kvindegaardslien. But we have all that we need for our daily lives.

Last month we had a visit from Halvor Kvindegaarden, I should greet you from him. He is plagued with many evil thoughts, it is sorrow upon sorrow, he says. He read your letter and read about Aagot. He had thought about writing to her but isn't good at it. He planned to stay here two days but it became almost a week. He saw that we have it good with good neighbors, all we need.

You must all now live and greet everyone we know and would like to hear from us. Loving greetings from me and mine. Clara now has a pen. She will write to Grandfather later.

Sigrid

2 ✒ LETTER FROM ANNA

Dear Grandfather,

Because I am the biggest and remember you the best,[1] I will send a letter to you to tell you about my siblings and myself.

First I will tell you that Micheal has now read in the Forklaring, and then we have read in the Bible History and are reading in the Testament. Then we have the Sunday School papers and newspapers. Micheal and Lars have the China Missionary paper. Last fall we borrowed one of Ole Skjervem's books and it was so much fun to read in that. Could grandfather please send one with Knud Jallo? Lars reads in the catechism, and Birgit[2] in the ABC. She spells and makes words. Clara is a little of each. She reads the ABC and sings a little of each song she hears from us. Thy Little Ones Dear Lord Are We, Deilig Er Den Himmel Bla,[3] etc. She is a good girl. You should

---

[1]Anna left Norway at age six, and was now age 13.
[2]Birgit or Birgita is Cecelia; her middle name was Birgitte.
[3]"How Lovely is the Blue Heaven"

hear and see her. I think you would like her. She is a comfort to us all. Papa and she are very good friends. One time she said she liked whiskers, butter and bread. I hear in your letter how cozy you have it. It would be good for us to get to go to school at your place and if we did that we would be satisfied—and we would really try to learn to read and be smart. It would be good if we could learn about Him wherever we wander in the world. From the boys I can send greetings and say they were both willing to be your shepherd boy, but then the way is so long, and in the summer we have it very busy because then we have English School and we have a great desire to go there.

We are striving to learn Geography and everything is fun. I get the most praise from the teacher and that is fun. Now I have written a long letter and with that I wish these well meant lines find you in the best of prosperity. I close my letter today and I am glad I have a grandfather in Norway who will remember me and my relatives in your prayers to God. Live well, everybody, Grandfather, Grandmother, Uncle—"mother brother," Nels, Knud and Ole. If it is possible, write to me also. I shall greet you from Micheal, Lars, Birgit, Clara and little brother.

Anna

I shall greet you from Birgita that she is good to take care of little brother and to read.

Lillehaugen
October 30, 1892

Dear parents,

One postday after the other has gone by without a letter
from you. It appears to me that I have been written down in
your forgotten book at your place. But to freshen your minds,
I am sending you a few lines. It could happen that it might interest you. You will hear from me that we are all in good health
and everything is well with us all, and it is a good gift and I am
heartily glad as long as we can have it so good, yes, God has to be
thanked for that. This summer we have had the best and nicest
weather, so for the first time we got a good crop.

Now we have threshed and plowed. Now they have left to haul
the wheat to town before winter comes, because then it is best to
hibernate like the bear. We got over 800 bushels of wheat, 400
oats. The wheat is worth 50¢ a bushel. Low price! Now we have to
sell wheat to pay for the horses we bought last fall for $200, and
threshing cost $52. We had a man during threshing for two dol-
lars a day. So that's the way it goes with the money. It goes here
and there. But we are satisfied that God has helped here. This
year I guess there has been very bad weather at many other places.
Through the summer we sold eight cattle. We have 22 left and we
have enough hay for them. We have mowed quite a bit, Micheal
has done most of the mowing and raking. Grandfather should
see how big and smart a man he has become this fall. Now he
is going along with Father and drive to town and they will both
have teams.

Lars has to watch the cattle and that is not so good now with
prairie fires all around the places. Theodore will now be one year

the 4th of November. He is so big and fat, everybody who has seen him says they have never seen such a fat baby child. He doesn't walk yet but crawls around everywhere.

Birgit and Clara have found pen and paper to write to grandfather but it probably won't be finished before tomorrow. Anna is now almost as big as I am. She can use my clothes. She is good. This summer she had to help with the haying and people from town came out and asked her to work for $3 a week. But we needed her. They are all a big help and comfort.

What has happened to Knut?[4] I have sent a letter to him in care of Uncle but I haven't heard a word from him. Is he in Norway again? Knud Jallo asks about him and you every time I talk to him. He says to greet you.

The ones I get a letter from are Sigri Sondreal and H. O. Kvindegaard. Both complain because you don't write to them and I do the same! I am waiting to hear from you, yes, dear Father, send us a long letter for Christmas. Today is All Saints Day and we have been to a meeting—everybody except Lars and Micheal. They were home.

Now I suppose you have started school and so have we. We have to begin with the Norwegian again during wintertime. Now I have to cut off this short letter with heartfelt wishes that these lines will get to you all dear people with best wishes for soul and body. We are all living well and send our dearest greetings to you and relatives and friends. Live well wishes your daughter and sister.

Sigrid L

---

[4]Knut Gjeldaker Nelson was living and working in Luverne, MN. He was visiting his uncle, *Store* Ole Nilsen, and working on farms in the area.

October 24, 1893

Dear Father!

Because yesterday I had the big satisfaction to get a letter from you I will send some words back to you in return. I thank you heartily for the letter and all the pictures. It was so much fun for us to see everybody again, Anna and I had often wished we could have pictures and now we got that satisfaction too. I hardly know my brothers again they have gotten so big and handsome men since I saw them. We have seen a lot since that time—both sorrows and joys. What you told about in your first letter brings sorrow—that Iver could be so tempted—that was too much. There are heavy days for you this fall and something that will never be forgotten, especially his family.

I think and dream about the situation and I can't imagine that mess. Gro—how does she take the sorrow and who gives her comfort? According to the way you wrote he must have gone insane so it was during insanity he did this terrible self-murder! Yes, it brings tears to read about sorrows of all kinds, but I suppose it is so that sorrow and gladness turn to hope.

Yes, dear Father, I got to know you now the way you are. I often thought of you as an old gray-haired man but now I see you are as young and handsome as you can be. Old age hasn't gotten hold of you yet. It is so good to see you this way.

I can tell you everything is well. Health is best of all. We have had a good summer as we got good crops.

We have a healthy baby boy born on September 5. Now on Sunday 22nd of October he was baptized and he got the dear familiar name, Nels. I like that. In one month there will be a meeting again and maybe it will be confirmation. If so, Anna will probably be confirmed, Sunday the 25th. After that she says she will send Grandfather a letter.

You say that Lars could come to you in school. If that were possible, the only thing is, I would want to be home so my children could be with you in school. I thank God that we have gotten us a home here where we have everything we need for daily bread. It is also a possibility that Lars could have a chance to learn here. The minister tells us we have children who are good in reading. They read at every meeting[5] in the summer. This summer we have had regular meetings every 3rd Sunday and this spring Tosten was chosen sexton for this congregation.

If I only had more melodies of Father because I teach Tosten all I can, so we have song school at home. Times are changing here for the better. People are beginning to settle up here. We have also gotten another quarter of land, namely, Homestead Land. We have filed and it cost $16. It is cheaper here to buy farms. We now have two quarters side by side. We have a new neighbor, namely, Sander Lofthus. They came this spring and bought a quarter of land. They have now built a house and moved in. Margit was with us two weeks. They now have one daughter left. Their two sons died right after they came here this spring, that was sad for them, and the people are kind to them. They have gotten three calves and Knud Lokken (or Turke Knud) feeds them three months for nothing. That was worth a lot of money to them. And still he gave them a calf and helps them in many ways, so they say they like it here, so I suppose they do.

We have nice weather up to this time and that's good for people who have to plow. You must live well. Yes, Father, Mother and brothers, and loving greetings from me and mine.

Yours, Sigri

---

[5] Worship service

I guess I'll send a few more lines hoping that you have received a letter with pictures that I sent to you this summer. Let me know if it has come or not. Around here the ones you know all have good health. I should give greetings from Knud Jallo and family. He would like to hear from you, also, we have a stranger from Iowa, namely Knud L. Nestegaard. He asked me to greet you so much, Father. News is so scarce there is nothing to write about except all is well. Micheal is now through plowing and he has plowed 40 acres almost alone with two oxen. Now it is to haul wheat to town but it is so sorrowfully cheap. Think, only 50¢ and less for each bushel. This fall we got 900 bushels wheat and 300 bushels barley and oats. We had a threshing machine one day for $60, so it is expensive work here in Dakota. There was a time this fall they paid $2 a day with the machines so the farmer has to pay a lot again. We bought a self-binder this fall and paid $130. From us they got four oxen, for which they gave $106, and the rest he paid with cash. You might know, grandfather, that Micheal was a big man when he got to sit on the new binder and drive it.

Father and Anna shocked so we do not have to hire anyone for work because the children are so big and strong that they work like grown people. So we have it good with that too lately.

The letter I had from Knud asks if I think he should come here and take land but I haven't heard from him for a long time.

I suppose you have heard Sigri Gudmundsrud[6] is married to Niels Svendsen. I will here cut off my letter. Greet everyone who wants to be greeted from me.

Sigrid

---

[6]Sigri was the daughter of Nils Nilsen Gudmundsrud and the Nils she married was a son of Gro Gudmundsrud Svendsen (Swenson). The two were first cousins, and each was a first cousin of Sigrid, the writer of the letters. The couple lived first at Northwood, ND, then at Fordville, ND.

Michigan City
December 3, 1893

Dear Grandfather!

If I could follow with the younger children and visit you
in these Christmas Holidays, oh! but that would be fun! But
because that isn't possible, with the pen's help I will send a few
words, because I hear you would like a few lines from me. So I
am going to see to it to fulfill your wish because that is all I can
do for you now, but news is lacking so this will be an odd letter,
for which I apologize.

First I'll tell you we are all living well and we all have our
health and my relatives are growing and thriving. As for myself,
I have come far enough in this world to be confirmed and that
was a festive day for me that I will never forget in my memory.
But it was one thing that was lacking. The minister asked me
for my baptism certificate and we did not bring that along from
Norway. But even if I am confirmed, I haven't quit the English
School because if I want to, I can go one or two years more. That
is the most fun I know. I would go all the time if I could, but I
must also be helpful at home because we have so much to do.

I am always healthy so it is fun to have something to do. I
have to tell you I got a nice Confirmation Memento from the
minister, and mamma gave me the picture of you that we got.
O! How glad I was for that. I have a nice album, which cost one
dollar, and you have the first place. From Birgit Svensen I got a
nice big book, On Special Prayers by D. L. Moody. She also sent
us a Salmodikon that we can borrow for awhile so now we can
learn to play and sing, but I guess papa will send for a new one
for us.

Now it is pretty soon Christmas and it is long to wait for us all because we get so many gifts. Yes, we have it good here. You could come and visit us and you would find peace with us and you could see the little ones here who call you "Gofa."

Theodore is a good little man. He knows your picture and calls you "Gofa." Lars must be like Nels Morbro[7] because Theodore calls him Lars. He calls Micheal Jaka. He can't say Micheal. Now this better be all for this time. I hope these simple but well-meant lines will find you in the best of health and that this will get there before Christmas. Live well and a Merry Christmas and a good new year I wish to you.

Your Anna Lillehaugen

[Upside down on original letter] Greet grandmother and Nels and Ole if they remember me. I am sending a little piece of my confirmation dress to grandmother with 1000 greetings.

6 ⌒ LETTER FROM MICHEAL

Michigan City, N.D.
Dec. 3, 1893

Dear Grandfather,

Because you would like to see my handwriting, I will try to send you a few lines, but I am a poor man to write because I don't have much time for that because I have to be with my father both summer and winter. Now we have much to do outside

---

[7]Mother's brother

but it has not been cold this winter. Just a little snow and no storms up to this time. We use the wagon when we go to town.

Tomorrow papa and I are going to town to sell wheat, which we hauled in earlier, but it is so little price for wheat. This fall under 50¢ a bushel. This fall we bought a new binder. It should cost $130 but they got four oxen. We sold them according to weight so we got $106. We also sold two cows and got $26 each. Because you can't see me, I have to tell you I have become big but not as fat as when you saw me. I am well grown and strong and I am never sick, which is good. It is soon Christmas and Mama has promised me something nice if I learn my lesson, and that makes me glad. Live well, then, dear grandfather. I hope you live long and happily.

Dearest greeting from your Micheal T. L.

7 — LETTER FROM SIGRID

This is Lars' side but because his writing is not good and he doesn't want Grandfather to see that so I will write a little instead. He will try and learn more another time. He envies Micheal because he thinks he will get a letter again and not Lars. Yes, it would be fun if Grandfather could send back a few lines. That would be heartily welcome for them. Yes, now you are getting a letter but it is well meant and you must excuse it.

I'll have to tell you about my girls. They are very kind—especially Clara. She is a comical little girl. I often wonder how long I can keep them. It is great that we can have them all around us, and everyone is healthy and intelligent. We thank God for all these gifts and think it would be fun if Grandfather could have them around him. But because that is impossible we will have to do it with the pen's help. All is well and we have to thank God and be satisfied and happy with each other. It is soon Christmas and then our thoughts more often would like to visit you. We remember our happy memories of youth always anew at this time. But all I struggle after now is to make our home cozy as we can to be together. And glad with each other. Yes, may God give us the right everlasting Christmas gladness. Live well, Father, and loving greetings I wish you all young and old. Live well.

Your Sigrid

8 ⌒ LETTER FROM SIGRID

Sunday, September 10, 1894

Dear Father,

Never before have I had you wait so long for a letter from me and I am really ashamed. I beg for your forgiveness. Therefore, I hope my lines will bring you a smile of satisfaction and happier thoughts when you have so much trouble and sorrow around you all over.

If information that has reached us is true, it has gone wrong with Knud E. Uff, that is sorrowful to hear. Here everything is well with us to date. If we can all stay well the time will go. We have now taken our crop.

It was about half as much as last fall but it is good we got something. Many got less than that this year because we had too little rain this summer, so many places it has been worse. We have an over supply of hay. We have put up well over 100 tons of hay and we have rented out just as much from the other quarter that we have taken as Homestead Land. We have broken up 40 acres this summer and built a little house there. We should now begin to live there but it is such a big expense to get houses for people and cattle.

All summer I have waited for Knud. He wrote and asked if there was work to get. It was very poor where he was, he said. I wrote and told him he should come because here daily wages were one dollar a day and 1½ dollars in harvest and threshing, but I am sorry that he didn't come. But he says he wants to see Dakota this fall. We would be happy if he would come.

Now Theodore and Nels and I are alone. Tosten and Micheal are in church. Anna has hired out one month for half dollar a day to cook for threshers for a threshing machine who boards them himself. Lars and the small girls watch the cattle for wheat stacks and hay stacks that are around here on the prairie.

There are people that have to haul their hay 20, 25, 30 miles. Our minister, who lives 13 miles from here, was here this summer and put up hay, and now he is hauling his own hay just like another farmer. He has four congregations to serve. This summer Missionary L. Skrefsrud was here to hold meetings. Anna got to go 20 miles to hear him. We have meetings every third Sunday in the summertime but in the winter it isn't that often.

This summer we had a visit from Svend A. H. and family and Gunder J. Skallehaugen told me to greet you and the family. His brother Kittel was killed one year ago this fall so there are many kinds of dangers for people.

Yes, now Theodore has written to grandfather. It looks like he can read some things but what he wrote here you can't understand, I suppose it is a greeting. He drives in his imagination all day long—horse and oxen. It would be fun if you could see all of my well-born children. They are so nice and kind. I hear others say so too. This summer five of them went to English School. Clara also wanted to be along. She was a small but intelligent pupil. She is five years this month. Nels has been sick the past two weeks but is better now. You are not getting a long letter this time but more later. Live well, dear Father, Mother, and greet everyone so heartily from us here.

Sigrid

9 — LETTER FROM SIGRID

August 1895

Dear Father,

I have been thinking about you many times and wanted to send some lines back to you so you can hear how things are with us. Many thanks for the long awaited letter, although it wasn't good, some of it, and we would have to take it with the best of meaning. I hear about grandmother, how burdened she is with arthritis and that is sad to hear, but it is lucky she got a room at your place, who are doing all you can for her, and she is patient to bear the trouble. I suppose in one way we all get it when old age comes.

Here with us everything is well. We are well every day and get along the best we can. We have had beautiful weather all through spring and summer. Everything looks so nice. We are almost through with the haying and are ready to take some wheat we seeded in March. Yes, now we have had a busy spring with moving and building a new house. In May we started tearing down the house and moving the lumber here. In June we got to move in the new house. We hired a carpenter one month for one dollar a day. It was cheap as he took a cow when he went, but now we have Knut L.[8] for hired man from May 1 for three months. He will also be here in harvest. Also for threshing.

We have now built three new buildings this spring. You see everything had to be new on the new land. A well with a pump and a pretty house with a big box for milk cans. There is room for 12 cans. The stable has three walls built up of stone and sod, the fourth one is boards with four doors and windows—about 30-40 pieces, so it was a big job. It was Tosten and Knut who built it. Now another well has to be dug also so we can get water inside during the winter. Yes, a lot of work has been done here this spring, and big cost, because you know we have to go to town for each thing we need, so we need a good crop to pay for everything this fall. We also had to buy another horse for harvest because we need three for the binder and we had to do away with one last fall. Now we got a pretty black mare for not quite $90.

This summer we have 11 milk cows but we have sold six cows, which will be delivered next week. I have heard from brother Knut. He has hired out where he is. So he will be in Minnesota. Knud K. Nedrebraten came up here with team from Minnesota and likes it. He is now hired man at Lars Skjervem. He is a good boy also. Niels Svensen and his wife and foster daughter visited us in July. They were here a week. Sigri had to come up to cook milk cheese. She didn't have a kettle and only two cows. Ole Sondreal came to O. Svenson. They are living well. Now three of the boys are married.

Grandfather, I suppose, is a painter yet. So you better come

---

[8]Knut Lillehaugen was a nephew of Tosten. Knut emigrated from Hallingdal to North Dakota in 1895. His brother Mikkel L. (sometimes called *Store* Mikkel) emigrated from Leveld in 1887, at age 21. Their brother Tosten S. Lillehaugen came in 1903. The latter two remained single. Mikkel died in a house fire in Whitman in 1929. Knut Lillehaugen remained in the area.

here and paint the house both outside and inside. We have nothing painted except one floor yet, and Anna and I did that. We have several rooms in the house yet to do, but this year we have to see that we pay for what we have done. I hope you can read my writing.

We sold a large bull this fall that weighed 1800 lbs.

10 — LETTER FROM SIGRID

16 September [1895]

Many days have gone by since I started this letter. It lay around like I did because August 11 I had a boy again. Everything is fine. We baptized him yesterday. Then he was five weeks and got the name Sigvald. Have you read about Sigvald Netland in the "China Missionary"? I hope you get that regularly.

We now have our grain in stacks. We have 27 stacks, really a big crop this year—much to thank God for, both inside and outside. But now folks always have something to complain about because it is such a poor price for wheat when there is so much of it.

The oats were about 70–80 bushels per acre and the wheat between 30–35, yes, and even up to 40 bushels, they say who have threshed it. Today I had to let Anna go out and help cook for the threshers. The woman she worked for last year was so anxious to have her again. They have now threshed two weeks. Both the Knuts are with them on the same machine.

All my children are fine. So am I. We live well every day. The young ones have gone to English school now for the last five months. Now it is over. Now the minister reads with the children through the summer. He likes Micheal so well. He is now reading with the confirmands. So time just rushes by when everything is well.

I am distressed about one thing in the letter you sent to Tosten. It is hard for you and for us to begin to pay on that old debt now when we are struggling here to get a home and build. That's all I can say. He will answer himself. Money isn't so easy to get.

Now this paper got too small. Now you must all live well. I wish for you.

Sigrid

11 ⌐ LETTER FROM SIGRID

March 14, 1896

Dear Father,

It wasn't too early if I, today, took time to answer your welcome letter, which is always so great to receive for all of us here, because your letters always bring such good exhortation. So today I can get permission to send you my greetings and say that everything is so well here with us and everyone has a greeting from us large and small. We have had an outstanding nice and mild winter and now it will be the approaching of the mild and delightful spring. I thank God for all good gifts and all the times He protects us so well. I often wonder how long we can enjoy these "Sunny Days."

We now have the satisfaction that Brother Knut[9] has come here, and for us it surely was a great comfort because he is a

---

[9]Knut Gjeldaker Nelson came at Christmas, 1895 from Luverne, MN, and stayed with Sigrid and Tosten for a time, soon obtaining land nearby.

handsome, big man and is good and kind—a good example for others. It is great for those who can be that and get away from many temptations from the Devil. Now he has been here and if it is anything to do outside or inside he helps. He helps the boys with ice-skating, and helps take care of the small boys. Sigvald and Nels often sit one on each knee, and I say he is now paying back an old bill that I lent him one time. And we are also satisfied about one more thing and that is he is going to take a quarter of land so we will be neighbors.

Now in February Micheal was at Knut Jallo. There was Norwegian School there for one month. Knut took his place here. Micheal is now going to read for the minister. He is so big— almost like Uncle Knut. This spring we will get two months Norwegian School and I am glad because it is such a kind and intelligent teacher. Then it will be four of ours. Theodore has also gotten an ABC and he spells and learns, then Nels can learn from him again. He also learns the alphabet at the same time, yet, it is so great that they can get understanding and have the capability to learn. You would also be glad in my children if you were here, dear Father. Knut often wishes for a picture of Sigvald, who is his favorite. Father should see them. If everybody is well next summer, perhaps it will happen.

It was funny to see you, Mother, again in Beihovd.[10] Uff, how many rocks there are. It is something to wonder about for people here. If you would also hold a horse with a collar on, it would have been still more strange.

Everybody greets you and will now send you a little memento in case it could interest them a little. By rights it should have come to you for your birthday. So my little letter must end and send over there our best wishes and greetings. Grandmother

---

[10]Referring to picture received.

is still with you and remembrance of her also as my good, old Mother. I hope she will soon get to sleep from her tired, wandering strife. Tomorrow Micheal and Knut will go to town with wheat.

Sigri

12 — LETTER FROM SIGRID

Lillehaugen
August 28, 1896

Dear Father,

It is a long time now since I sent you a greeting so now I am finally going to get a letter sent. I can let you know that we are all healthy to date and that is a good thing if we can at all times keep our health. Now I will tell you how the time goes. Today, for example, Micheal is at the minister's for confirmation this coming Sunday. Anna went with him so our thoughts and memories are with you wishing you could be here on Sunday, too. Lars is now out to try out the mower. He was along this summer to plow so now he is grown up from herding. Now it is the girls' job to herd. Theodore and Nels are often along so that leaves Sigvald and me alone inside. He is beginning to stumble and walk. He is intelligent. He also says many words. What was he created for? His name in China is, "His lot is a mournful message."

We are almost through with our haying, and then they have the harvest, so that is where most of the time will go. It is left a little wheat and oats. We have a poor crop. The crop is about half of what we got last year. They are talking about 15 bushels an acre. We are satisfied, therefore, and thank God that He let us keep that. There has been damage many places this summer. We had hail four times this summer, but a stretch south and north it hailed out for many of them. They have only plowing left. It is sad to see something like that. We drove to Lakota a week ago after the storm and we saw the same kinds of fields there.

We are not having school this summer. We had Norwegian School this spring and this fall there will be English School. A little about the Norwegian School might interest you, grandfather. We had an intelligent teacher who had attended Sogndal High School. His name is Andrew Berdal. He was here and boarded when he was closest to the schoolhouse two miles from here. I had to send lunch for eight to school every day—four of ours, two from Knut Jallo—another girl and the teacher. Then it was school in the other school four miles from here. Then Micheal drove every day and then there were often seven—eight in the buggy with two horses ahead. Then Tosten was so kind because he hired a man instead of Micheal so he got to go to school every day and he is so anxious that the children will learn and that is our duty also for them, but how many can we find in this land who are careless about this? Now it is a boy 10-11 years old who is with the confirmands but it is uncertain if he will be confirmed. He hardly knows the five parts of the catechism. When school was out this spring, the teacher asked the children if they would promise him to learn one question every day and not put the books aside.[11] We hope to get him again next spring, but he is so taken up with school, so he said he would try to help out all he could, but now Lars has become so intelligent he got a desire for the book.

---

[11]The Explanation book, used to prepare for confirmation, was written in the form of questions and answers. Students memorized the answers and corresponding Bible verses.

He is now happy he is on the fifth part of the catechism and they finished the first part. Cecelia is studying the second article, and Clara is learning the catechism by heart. They all want to learn the most until Berdal returns. It has always gone good with Lars but he is simpler and doesn't advance as quickly as Micheal, who is more like an 18 year old.

A news item from here—Ronaug Lofthus was married in July to Nels Nelsen Mork from Hol—an old man, but it was O.K. anyway, because he had many horses, cows and several hundred sheep, so now there will be big fuss over at Margit Bjella again. They had a big wedding. Many were invited. They got over $60 in the dish. They were allowed to have the party at Lars Skjervem's because he had just built a new barn 60 feet long and 36 feet wide. There was a dance Saturday night.

Sunday night we had the worst storm we have seen in Dakota with lightning, thunder and rain, but first came a terrible storm that blew over many small houses and some big ones here and there. Skjervem's barn blew into pieces, so now it is on the ground in small pieces after just one storm.

I suppose you heard I had company of boys here this summer. It was Nels Svendsen who brought his uncle here, *Store* Ole Gudmundsrud, father's brother, but they were here only one night. It was strange to see a big old man so like Grandfather. I have had a letter from him since he was here, and then he sent me the last letter from you that we got to see. When you get freed from school half a year, you will come here and visit, won't you? We talked to Aagot Skrinde after she was in Norway again. She had greetings from you, and you had said you would like to see America.

What is the address for Uncle Knut? If you will, please send me his address.

Monday, August 31

Now I have to send my letter and tell you about yesterday. It was a festival day for all of us. Yes, we had such a good confirmation meeting as it could be. It was a good sermon. It was Ringstad, and he was so good to talk. We surely got to hear our duties as parents, and fulfilling our duty in bringing up a child, and, even if we do our best, we have to do more and be responsible. So we got to hear that, also. For me, this day will be long remembered. It isn't often people need to feel tears, but yesterday many did.

From Knut I can greet you and say he lives well. He followed us from the meeting and got dinner and two of his friends. He got such good dried pork. He hadn't tasted it better than that since he ate it at Father's. This summer we have had fifteen cows but now we traded one away for a buggy, and Svend Nestegaard is going to have one of them, because he has been here and painted our house.

Two brothers of Ole Nestegaard came here this spring from Iowa and one from Jermund Sando. They have all taken land around here, so now the land is being taken up fast. Knut has probably told you that he will be our neighbor. Now the threshing has begun, and Anna has gone out to cook for them. No, now I'm beginning to bore you.

Next time we have a meeting we will have a visit from the minister and his wife. I wish you could be here now. Tomorrow I am going to Ladies Aid at Knut O. Loken, or, rather, his wife. There aren't too many of us, but we are good. So I send my loving greetings. Greet relatives and friends.

From Lars I shall greet you that today he studied his Explanation.

Sigri

14 ⌒ LETTER FROM KNUT

Michigan City
December 6, 1896

Dear Father, Mother, and Brothers,

Now it is time to send you a few words so you will get it for the New Year. I first have to tell you I'm living pretty good, and, as I told you in my other letter, I am staying with my sister because my thoughts were to go to English school, but then things changed my figuring. Winter came one month too early and they had to close the school. They couldn't bring the little ones to school in the cold and all this snow on the prairie. When it blows one can't even be out so that was my schooling again, but I could go to school in town, but that costs money and it isn't so much of that here in Dakota either. As I have already said— winter came too early for many—yes, entirely too early because there are many who haven't threshed, and many had thought of building more and preparing better, but the snow wouldn't wait till they were done. A few days ago we had a terrible blizzard for four days. It blew and snowed so all that time. Some people tied a string to the corner of the house so they could find their way inside again. Yes, that was the worst snowstorm I've ever seen since I came to America, and I hope I never see it again. We cannot get out now without clearing the road.

Now we have gotten a new president again and the old party, namely, Republican, or the money powerful, lost this year, but next time, namely in 1900, we will shout hurrah for W. J. Bryan. That is the candidate for president for the workers. This year he had 22 states and the other, namely, McKinley, had 24. He just about won. I must close for this time with a loving greeting to you all and it is my heart's desire that these lines find you in the best of health. I wish you all a Merry Christmas and a Happy New Year.

Your son and brother,
Knut L. Nelson

I mustn't forget to thank you for the letter you wrote in Vester-heimen;[12] yes, it was right it came in there.

Will you be so kind and send my Uncle's address, Mother's brother. I have written to him but no reply before I wrote Myking.

15 — LETTER FROM SIGRID

December 8, 1896

Dear Mother!

Now that Knut is writing to Father I will send a few lines to you. You haven't gotten many letters from us since we left. I hope it reaches you in your dear home and I wish you the best of everything. We here are living quite well and I thank our God.

---

[12]Newspaper

We have now for a long time felt troublesome about Little Nels because he was so unlucky the 27th of October. He was in a prairie fire and became terribly burned.[13] His face and hands, especially his right. It was a terrible time for us all, but worst for him, poor thing. The doctor was here four times, and he saw what we knew, that he couldn't stand that awful pain. But now he is better. You can believe we were afraid for him the first week. Think, if he had been impaired from it, but to our joy he was saved. It was because he had been sleeping when the fire came over him. His whole help was that he was wearing wool. All his clothes had fire on them earlier. Yes, it was terrible, but it could have been worse. It is not certain how it will go with the hand—if it will be entirely all right again, because all the fingernails fell off at first. The doctor said we had to go to the hospital with him, because he thought it was worse than it really was, but then the boy became so sick and we couldn't even get to town with him. For two weeks he didn't eat and then he had a little milk, but then it was only water he wanted because he was also burned in his mouth, because he had it open when he was sleeping, poor boy. Now his face is marked up so he won't be like he was before. But we give God a big thank you that it didn't get worse than it did.

Now comes Sigvald clear up to the table to me.

Now it is soon Christmas. It gets talked about a lot these days. Everybody waits for it. I have to brew yet and soak Christmas Fish because we have a little Norwegian food for Christmas

---

[13] While Tosten and Micheal were fighting the prairie fire, three-year-old Nels followed without their knowledge. He became tired, lay down in the tall grass, fell asleep, and the fire swept over him. Nels bore the marks of his tragedy for the rest of his life. Nevertheless, Nels played the violin, enjoyed hunting, and was interested in photography. He used a camera with glass negatives, developing his pictures in a dark room, transferring many of his pictures onto post cards. In February, 1915, without telling his parents, he went to Fargo to undergo surgery on his face. He died on the operating table from an overdose of chloroform.

if that is right. I now have a cow that milks and Lars milks her, so I am not in the barn once a week either. We have so much extra work with Nels. Now we have to bandage him once a day with cotton and salve. It's healing fast now, so we hope he will be well by Christmas. Anna is having a quiet winter at home. She is gone once in awhile, but I like it best when she is home. Now till Christmas she has a lot of clothes to sew, if we shall have a garment.

Tomorrow I am going to Kristi Nestegaard to Ladies Aid. Now I will have to quit for today and send my loving greeting to you and all of yours. I wish you a Merry Christmas and a Happy New Year.

Your Sigrid

16 ⌒ LETTER FROM ANNA

Michigan City, N. Dak.
Feb. 18, 1897

Dear Grandfather!

Now it is long since I have written to you and I have earlier had the joy of reading three of your letters that you sent, so now I will send you a few lines so you can hear how we have it here on the prairie and how we all are. Nels is almost well again. He still has a small sore on his forehead, and he will have big scars over his whole face for awhile, but he is so young that I think he will outgrow it.

It is good he got to keep his eyes undamaged. But his right

hand doesn't look so good, but with God's help, it can also be well again. It won't be much for me to write about when all the others write also, but I haven't much to say as I am home all the time and help mamma, but maybe it would interest you to hear a little about Theodore and Sigvald when they can't write themselves. Theodore is five years and most of his work is reading. It is easy for him to learn. He has now learned the ABC book once and has started it again. Sigvald is a good little boy and a dear.

It gladdened us a lot to read your letter and see how much you got done there at home. My thoughts about you came. It would have been nice to be with you there and we would be happy with you all. But since we can't do that I will take my pen and send you my heartiest wish for happiness.

We heard in Vesterheim that you are speculating about taking a trip over here. Oh, yes, are you doing that? Then you would be kind. It would be great to see and hear you over here with us and it would gladden many others to see you.

Last Sunday we were at church in the schoolhouse because we have worship in the schoolhouse. We saw K. Jallo and he told us to greet you so much. Papa and Mamma also send you their loving greetings. I must close my letter for this time. Please excuse my disconnected letter but we must remember I haven't gone to school at Grandfather Gjeldaker. Greet grandmother and Morbror so much from me, but first and last you are heartily greeted from me. Greet everyone who remembers me. Live well.

Anna Lillehaugen

Dear Grandfather,

Now that I have just turned 10 years, I will try to write a few words to you so you can see my simple writing. We have no other school than what Papa and Mamma give us, and then we read the Testament, so now I am on the third Article. In Bible History I read in the book. In March the English School begins again. Then I read the third book. I also read in three other books, too. You maybe don't like to bother with my letter, so it's best to close with my best greetings to Gofa and Gomo Gjeldok from me.

Cecelia Lillehaugen

Dear Grandfather,

Because I am a little girl of seven years this letter will not be long. I write big, but Mamma thinks you will excuse me and think about I'll get better with time. I read every day, even if we have no other teacher but Papa or Uncle when he is home. I must quit my little letter. I am afraid you cannot read my writing. Live well and greet everyone.

Clara Andrea Lillehaugen

Dear Grandfather,

When the others are writing to you, I will also write you a few lines, although I am a poor writer, but I hope to get better later. But it is uncertain to be like you for then I should be in school, but I am now helping with the cattle because Micheal goes often to town, because we now have such a good road to town, because we have so much snow this winter. So now I have to say goodbye and send hearty greetings to you all from me.

Lars Lillehaugen

Dear Grandfather!

Also a greeting from me so you know I am well and haven't forgotten you. I want to congratulate you on the medallion you received.[14] We were so happy to hear about it, even if we couldn't participate in the Fest they held for you. Tomorrow Uncle Knut and I are going to town with wheat. It is now a better price. It is about 61¢ a bushel. I must close my little letter for this time with a loving greeting from me.

Micheal Lillehaugen

---

[14]Lars Gjeldaker received the King's medal when he retired from teaching.

21 ⟋ LETTER FROM SIGRID

Many thanks for the letter. I would be so happy to own your picture.

Live well, from your
Sigrid

22 ⟋ LETTER FROM SIGRID

August 12, 1898

Often remembered Father!

Many times in my thoughts I have written to you but I haven't had time. But I think it is so seldom we send our thoughts ahead. If we would be near enough we would have much to talk about, but now it only gets to be letters. Now I want to tell a whole lot about us here. Yes, we live well every day and are healthy, and each one has his work to do—little and big.

The crop looks nice. We haven't been hurt by hail to this time. It has been hail in the west and north of us that has done a lot of damage. August 12 today Micheal has cut our barley. They are almost done with haying. We need 100 loads for winter.

The letter you sent to Knut for his birthday in February I have read it also with happiness and thanks to God because He is so good to us to this time. What the future brings, we will see later.

Today I am home alone with the youngest. The others are at a meeting. Lars, Cecelia and Clara are reading for the minister because it is too little Norwegian School among us here, but we have the good luck that they are all so intelligent and well liked both by the minister and teacher. I am writing this to make grandfather happy to hear how intelligent they are at this time in the English School. The teacher they have now says Cecelia should be a teacher, and, if we want to, she will take her along with her this winter, but she wants her to read Norwegian during the winter. Now they have had four months in English School, and they have come a long way both in reading and writing. Both Cecelia and Clara are in division in the arithmetic book. Now the sixth of August it was the last day, and then it was a fest for the children and the parents were invited. There were 66 people there. Clara counted them. Then they took pictures of the children and the teacher. Clara then was up and spoke, as they say here, and got applause so that it rang in the schoolhouse. The children sang one English and one Norwegian song. The girls had sewed a bedspread, which they gave to the teacher. It was welcomed with heartfelt feelings because she didn't know anything about it, so she was surprised. The teacher said to me that we must let Lars go to school in the winter. He is the kindest boy in the whole school and it has over 20 children. He was fussed over by all the people. That must be because he is Lars! He was well liked in Norwegian School in the winter. "Lars is so kind." We heard this about him from the people. You should see Selma now. She has grown a lot so it looks like she will soon walk and she is not ten months yet, yes, it is good they are all healthy and well born. We are yearning so for Vesterheimen so long as the history of the minister lasts.

I still have more to write about. June 15 there was a fest here because we had an auction. The Ladies Aid fed the people. It was eight members and we sold for $81 that day—$50 cash and the rest in the fall. There were many people and everybody got a free dinner. We women treated that. The minister was here also and two children of Sven Huus. Lina and Andrew were here, too. July 16 some of us from Pastor Ringstad's congregation surprised him and his wife with gifts, which cost almost $40. There were ten wagon riders in the group. When we got to the minister's home he was so puzzled when so many of us came. Schoolteacher Berdal was there, too. The minister got a pair of horse saddles and Mrs. got a rocking chair. We had a cozy meeting there, but hope and sorrow stay together. It is getting worse and worse with this church strife, which began when I last wrote to you. O. L. Nestegaard wrote a letter to the congregation, who wrote against him and wanted to write to the paper again, but the editor wouldn't print any more letters, but now he is writing one letter after the other embarrassing the congregation's people. Earlier he and a couple of others split from this congregation. So now we are pretty small who are standing by behind our old minister, who has served this congregation for 13 years and almost no pay. Now O. L. N., Sander Lofthus, and Jens Helland have a new minister from the synod and are trying to get a congregation started. On Sunday they got eight members, so it will be a big congregation then. They also split up our little Ladies Aid. We were eight, and now we are four on each side. We will work for a new church. It is sad that our own district people should act this way. Now we can have neither school nor church together.

Excuse this, Father, that I'm dwelling on this. Rather, now you will hear about Knut Brother. He left us the first part of April and was gone until June. Then he stayed with us for two weeks again while he was resting. He lived on his land and got J. O. Sando to break up a few more acres. He has a little house there. Stove, table and bed he had to have. It can maybe be enough work now if he works for the man he did last summer. Now he has been here with us but he doesn't have to pay one cent because we have food. As long as Tosten likes him, his home is here, and when Knut is hardworking and agreeable he often talks with Tosten about this and that.

Now, goodnight, Father. Greet everyone.

Anna has hired out in threshing. She gets $1 a day. Knut Lokken, *Turke Knut* in Norwegian.

Live well.
Sigrid

23 ✒ LETTER FROM SIGRID

November 30, 1898

Dear Parents,

Now that Knut has a letter ready to you and tomorrow Tosten goes again, the letter must go so you get it for Christmas. Yes—for Christmas! That word brings many thoughts to life—both for the past and now. It is especially about Christmas at your place that brings the dearest memories. Now it will be merely thoughts to relive again of the times of long ago. I have so many things to thank you both for, and also God, who has, up to now, taken care of everything so well for me & mine, and health is most important of all. What God gives us is much to thank for. Our family is now large, but God gives us regular care for our daily living, so then it is easier to be parents. We don't suffer for lack of food or clothes. It takes a lot in a year, but also many take part in the work.

Now we hope that Knut would be here again both for his land and earlier, so we could send one of the boys to school, so the lot fell on Micheal, for Lars is not through with confirmation yet.

Micheal got a place in town. He works for his board and room for a butcher, and then it is to pay for the school money and books, but he has not gotten to begin school. I was in town yesterday and talked to them and they like it well. The school needs them and it is good when they can make use of the time.

Right here at home all is well, except Selma isn't feeling too well now, but I hope she becomes well again. The rest are healthy as junipers.

Father, I have to give you a compliment for your last letter. When people see your unusually beautiful handwriting and hear your age, they break out with compliments about you. Then you know I bring out the other letters and your picture. When I got your letter there were between 15 and 20 threshers here, mostly Yankees, but the letter was passed around the whole house before I had the chance to open and read it. So there were many good words passed around.

I will write a bit about threshing. They began here 15 of October and left again Sunday morning. Then they had threshed 2500 bushels. Pretty good! Tosten then paid the workers a sum of almost $100, so it is expensive. One of our neighbors paid $300 and another one $600. Today we have butchered two pigs. Tomorrow we will take three sheep so we can get dried meat.

Now Selma is calling Mama so I shall close this letter, and I hope this simple letter will find you all well, and hope you all will have a Merry Christmas together and think about us here. We again gather our thoughts and hope your happiness will last. That is my wish tonight.

Live well, everybody, and I mustn't forget dear old grandmother. Her cross is long and heavy, but our good God watches over her all her days.

Greetings from Sigrid and everyone. Merry Christmas.

Sunday, 3 of May 1899

Dear Parents and Siblings!

Also a few lines from me. It has been awhile since I had your dear letter. I send my most sincere thank you to receive a letter reporting that all is well. I can report the same to you, because we are living as before—all well with the health and all we need to uphold us. We here have had a good winter and good spring. After 14th of April we have had no hay for the cows and it is one month normally yet. Here there are many green acres to see in the next week also to seed. Now it will be the third time we buy seed.

Just so we are lucky to get a crop. Awhile back we had a visit from a newcomer from Ål. It was Ole T. Rodningen. He could tell us a little about you because he had talked to you, Father, and he knew he would soon meet us. I heard then that Sigri Gudmundsrud wanted to come here in the spring. Heard from Birgit Svensen. Hope these lines come through. Will you send me a pair of wool cards so then you will be very kind. I have worn mine out. Around here the people live in the hope that next year will be a good year.

I will have to end this and I hope you are getting along well. Heartiest greetings from me and all mine. The small girls greet Gofa and Gomo. Clara is now so clever to speak.

Your own
Sigri

Sarnia, N.D.
October 8, 1900

Dear Parents,

Your dear letter has been received for which I thank you. I see you all are healthy and that is good to hear. I can say it is the same from this side. I see in your letter you had a good year. It was the opposite here. It was so dry that not much grew. Then we got rain and everything grew so fast and that was a satisfaction to see and things looked better. The grain was almost ripe, then we had a terrible hail storm that took everything totally so we didn't get one kernel of wheat so we are having a hard time—as well as with the hay, and we need quite a bit of that now as I now have three horses and a colt, so I surely got right into it the first year as a farmer. We will have to live in hope that next year will be better. Just so we can get something to seed again. Tosten has cut a little wheat and still has some old wheat so he is satisfied.

Well, enough of that, because we are not alone in the storm. It took a piece 14 miles wide and 30 miles long. In some places it took big houses but mine was all right, except my shanty rolled over, but there was little damage.

Big Uncle has now visited us again and it was a great satisfaction to see and talk to him, because now I can say that I have also been in Norway. He gave such good information. Yesterday I took him to town again because he wanted to go down to Northwood. Even Gudmundsrud[15] was with him. In town he met an old friend, namely, Grete Johan, an excellent meeting. Uncle

---

[15] Later used the name Even Nelson.

went over and greeted him. At first Johan didn't know him but then Uncle said, "Don't you know Big Ole?" but then the tears weren't far away. After a little pause they had a long visit you can understand. Uncle is a helpful man who stands ready to help when help is needed.

This summer I was out and visited my uncle[16] and found him in pretty good condition. I also met Levor Stave, so you can send greetings to Knud his brother from me and say I have seen and talked to him.

So, in closing, all on Gjeldok are heartily greeted from me,

Your affectionate son,
Knut L. Nelson

26 — LETTER FROM SIGRID

Sarnia
9 October 1900

Dear Father,

I have to get a letter to you again because I have just had the happiness of receiving a letter from you. First, I want to say thank you for my letter and earlier for the girls' letters. They will write themselves in their own time. Oh, Father, I wished for you here the 27th, because it was the funeral for our dear little Amanda. She got to trade her home here with us for a better home up there. She died the 24th and was buried the 27th in the new cemetery two miles from us. She was six months and 11

---

[16] The Mykings at Brinsmade, ND.

days. She was healthy and fat way until August 5th. Then she got something called Summer Complaint. She became well again two times, then became sick again, and the doctor came and gave her medicine, but little or no help. Fortunately we were so ignorant and we wished her back. This separation time is bitter but, anyway, now we thank our God who came and took her from her suffering. Now it's a question if we can live so we can meet again. There came so many people here that day so it was 19 riding rigs in procession. The pastor talked here at home and earlier by the grave where she is now resting. She had a white coffin we bought in town for nine dollars. I could write a lot about that little one—how kind and good she was, but you already know that. It was a light rod we got this time. Who will be the next one—whose turn will it be?

You ask about Ringstad, where he is. He is a minister at United Church but both these years he has not come to the annual meetings, so therefore he can't take part in discussions, but both years he brings greetings to us from our Uncle Minister.[17] What they have against him is not a valid reason. They are envious because he came to either our home or Skjervem when he came west because he lives 12 miles farther east where he has three congregations. The fourth one he turned down because it was too much for him. Then it became a split in the congregations—where the church should be. The minister went with the ones who moved and then he bought a quarter of land, so now he has a farm if times get hard and they can't pay him. He has a living anyway and doesn't have to beg.

We have to try to get along because we won't have any crop, but we were lucky to have a little left from last fall, so we will have a living for this winter. But it is so much rain that it is so hard to

---

[17]Rev. Ole Nilsen was a brother of Sigrid's father. He served as a pastor at Scandinavia, WI. In 1920 he retired to Grand Forks, ND.

make the hay. We sold ten head this fall but we will have over 30 head to feed this winter anyway—besides, eight horses they need a lot of hay. We won't get much straw either, but we will have to hope for a nice winter. Then the cattle can feed themselves.

We have just sat and talked with *Store* Ole.[18] It was so much fun. We would have liked to have him stay longer.

Live well, then, dear Father and Mother. We didn't have a picture made of our little one.

Sigri and family

27 ⌒ LETTER FROM ANNA

Sarnia, N. Dak.
February 18, 1901

Dear Grandfather,

Because mama is going to write to you, I send a little greeting. It has now been several months since I received your letter that you are thanked for. It always makes me happy to receive a letter from Grandfather, for then I see he remembers me yet through his good and long letter. Here we all live well and have our health every day and then the time goes by so fast it is almost impossible to follow along.

This winter we are all home except Lars. He is about 18 miles from here and goes to school. He was home the first part of December and has been home one time since. We thought he might have gotten lonesome because he had never been away

---

[18] *Store* Ole was Ole Nilsen Gudmundsrud, a brother of Sigrid's father.

from home so much, but he said he liked it both at school and where he stayed. He has to be diligent and fast because the lessons are so long he hardly gets through with the lessons until 11 o'clock in the evening, he says. The other children are busy with the Norwegian books. The older have to teach the younger and they know that Papa and Mama will have to listen to them once in awhile to see if they have learned anything. In the summer Pastor Ringstad gives them lessons and listens to them next time there are church services. However, this winter it has been so much snow and storms that church services have been very irregular. The first part of March the English School will begin.

We have also had company lately. It was Ole and Birgit Myking and Knut and Aagot Myking. They were here for a week. Aagot's parents and relatives live well and have their health. They have it real nice to be new settlers. We were west and visited them last summer. There are quite a few of our relatives and friends around there.

Knut and Micheal's jobs now are mostly to shovel snow and haul straw and tend to the cattle. They say it won't be much hay left if it is a late spring because this winter began so early.

I shall greet you from little Selma because she can't write herself. She got the place as "little girl" again because little Amanda left us. Selma is growing big even if she is "little girl." I am afraid that this letter is of little interest to you. Excuse me and I will see if I can do better another time.

A loving greeting from,
Anna

P. S. Greet grandma so much, also Nels and Ole. Also everyone who remembers me. If you will write to me when you have time, your letter will be lovingly received.

Sarnia, P.O. N. Dak.
February 19, 1901

Dear Parents!

Because sister left this space for me I can also send you a thank you for your last letter, which I received earlier. I send you my best greetings. Because both sister and Anna have written, they have given you all the news about what is going on in the neighborhood. So this will have to be all for this time.

From your son,
Knut L. Nelson

Feb 1901

Dear Father!

I guess it was too long this time before I answered you when I got your dear letter for which I thank you. It is a joy to receive a letter when all is well on both sides. The same joyful message can I give you again, that we thank God for our good health and well being. We have it good compared to many of our neighbors. It has been a hard winter for those who don't have anything to burn and give the cattle because, up to now, it has been a tough winter with a lot of snow and here where hay was destroyed by hail. Yes, it is good we don't need anything in this life's needs. So it's good to help others a little which I thank God for.

Anna has written everything so I only have to add a few remarks. Then I think you would rather hear about Lars. He is now away at school this winter and likes it a lot. There are more than 200 students, six teachers and ten classes. Lars began the 6th and when he had gone three weeks he was through and went up to 7. I am bragging but it is good they can make use of schooling when they have a chance. From Theodore I can greet Grandfather and say that he now reads in the old Knudsen's Bible History.

I think the same as you, Father, that our Lord showed His plan this fall when He took again our little Amanda, and I say just like you that next time He wants one again we should be prepared for those tidings.

We had the joy this year for our children to be along at a Christmas Tree Fest, which was so cozy. It was the first time I saw a real Christmas tree.

December 3 we attended a wedding. It was at Skjervem. It was Knut S. Lillehaugen and Gunhild Skjervem. A pretty wedding and a pretty pair, too. This is all the news I have to tell you this time, so I will say farewell to you.

Greetings to you and all of yours.

Your Sigrid

Sarnia
June 8, 1901

Dear Father,

I just received your letter and hear that Grandmother has died. It is good to hear her pains have ended and we hope she got everlasting life and is saved. Yes, it was good for you people and the very best for her. It was a painful sickness and took a lot of nursing, so you probably thought it was nice to rest. So it is Sigri again who needs care and nursing. Who will it be that takes that cross? I suppose it didn't affect her when Mother was gone.

I would also like a little thing for a remembrance if there is an opportunity to send it to me. For instance a book, or a table-cloth or a shawl.

Here we are living as before. There is nothing new since I last wrote, except now we had a frost here and the small seed froze. The potato grass and wheat—I guess we are too far north sometimes.

These last days we had a visit from Birgit T. Kjeldergaard. She is also in North Dakota. The boys are now through in the field. Knut finished yesterday so now he can write to you himself. Live well for this time. Greetings from us all.

From your Sigrid

As you see on the power of attorney paper I have chosen you, Father, to act for me. If you would rather not, I give you permission to get someone else in your place.

Sigri [signed]
And Tosten [signed]

Sarnia
September 2, 1901

Dear Father,

I have thought of sending you a few lines for so long so you can see how we are living here. Yes, thank you, we are all well, and we have been so busy, and will be that way until threshing is done. Yes, this year we really got something to thresh. The crop this year is worth two years of crop, so we got a crop for this year and last year. We thank God for that. The summer has been unusually nice without storms that amounted to anything. Once in awhile it was very warm so now wheat is cut excepting the flax, of which there is a lot this year.

Today they began threshing in the neighborhood. New threshing machine and new threshers this year because J. O. Sando, Knut Lillehaugen and H. L. Skjervem bought a rig together. But this fall it cost $2,600, an entirely crazy world. Isn't that so? Brother and Lars went there today with each getting four dollars a day for man and team. It's a lot to pay for help now days. Micheal has hired out to another machine to be fireman. That is to watch the fire so the water boils all the time. Anna is with another machine again and makes food or cooks as they say here. She has seven dollars a week. There are two. Caroline Jallo is also going along. Clara is babysitter at Mrs. K Lillehaugen so my help has shrunk now for awhile. This summer Knut has also for the first time cooked for himself and lives on his land. He says to greet you and say he is too busy to write yet, but you will get so much more this fall and winter. He had bad luck this summer with his colt because it died. Knut felt very sorry then, but now he has made a lot of hay, and he is going to build his house bigger till you come and visit him.

I can now greet you, Father, from Pastor Skattebol. He was around here in Sarnia again to preach in the Synod Church, but they were unlucky because the church was damaged by lightning that struck the steeple and several other places. It cost $2,025 to get it repaired again. Skattebol then had to preach in the schoolhouse. It was the 16th of July we heard him, but at the same time there were services in the Zion Church in Ringstad's parish. It was 17th and 18th of July and a good meeting. Eight ministers were there, three Synod ministers preached, and it was good to see and hear everything. It was a comfortable meeting and many good speakers, so I think it will remain a memory for a long time in afterthoughts.

From Lars I can greet you. He is sending a picture of himself and two school friends. Can you recognize him? Perhaps Uncle Nels wants to see the picture, then send it back, he begs. Grandfather probably has one already.

So now you must all be greeted from us here. I hope to get a letter from you soon again. Live well and don't forget to write.

Your Sigrid

32 ⌒ LETTER FROM SIGRID

Sarnia
December 10, 1901

Dear Father,

It is not my turn to write a letter, but I have a desire to write a letter too, when I see all the others writing letters. You are about the only one I write to. I hope you can tell it by my writing, but

I hope you will forgive me and put on your glasses and read my lines, even if they are simple. We are all well and have our health and everything we need for this life. We had a good crop this year and a nice fall. The cattle go outside and almost feed themselves. Just a little snow so the sleigh can barely be used without a load, so then it is not deep.

Knut is a good man but he isn't writing to you. He says he will write when he has more time. Now he has left with Carl A. Nelsen to Northwood to celebrate Christmas together with relatives. Carl was here a week ago. There were a lot of questions about the Old Country but he was kind to give his messages.[19] Knut got a full house with wheat this fall, so he didn't have a house to live in this winter, so he had to move out. He got someone to take over his horses so he left.

27th of October we had a confirmation meeting, and Cecelia was confirmed with two other girls.[20] It is not a big congregation since there was a split. Here in the neighborhood the people are living well, except Sander Lofthus has lain sick for awhile, so now Knut has come home and helps there.

Here everyone has come home since I wrote to you last. Many were gone trying to earn money. Micheal was gone two months, and then he had made almost $100, and Anna almost as much. It is good wages in threshing time. In winter they will be home because we have so many cattle, because this fall there was no one who wanted to buy cattle. There were other things to live on.

Last time I wrote to you, I sent a picture to you. Lars is waiting for one back, you know. Now it will soon be Christmas and then

---

[19] Carl Adolf Nelson was a son of *Store* Ole, and a brother to Christopher Theodore, who married Cecelia Lillehaugen. Carl and *Store* Ole had just returned from a visit to Norway.
[20] Ragnild Skjervem and Amalia Moen.

you should visit us. I think it will be a quiet Christmas around here because many go out East. They get money to travel this fall. Yes, may they have good fortune in their travels.

Because I don't have anything interesting to write about to you, it is better to quit before you get tired of reading this. A loving greeting to you all from me with my family, and a Merry Christmas fest I wish you.

Your humble daughter,
Sigri L.

33 ⟋ LETTER FROM ANNA

A Merry Christmas and a Happy New Year I wish you all.

From, Anna

34 ⟋ LETTER FROM SIGRID

April 23, 1902

Dearest Father!

I now have two letters to answer you and thank you, thank you for both, and all the pictures. I have been so busy showing the pictures to the Hallings and the Valdreser. Everyone says they are so nice, but I think I enjoyed them the most. Knut got Sundre, Lars, Gofa and Uncle. Anna got Nels and Knut, so I have two left. Lars was going to write himself, but you will have to excuse him today because today is spring's work and then it is to plod in the field and say "giddap" to the horse. It is English they talk to the horses, you know.

People are beginning to talk about a late spring. It is so cold and it is very little seeded around here because it was so little plowed last fall, so people are now planting without plowing, but that is not our farming. Nelsen came back first part of April from his long visit in the forest.[21] He was so fat and red-faced just like he had been in Hallingdal. Yes, the next trip he will take will probably be home.

Six of our children are at the doctor today. They were vaccinated and have to show their pimples. There is talk about smallpox here so it is best to be vaccinated if it can help. It was school here, but they had to quit early because none of the children were vaccinated except Lars. Yes, six of my children went to school. Lars, 18 years, Sigvald, 7—all were well liked, and oh so good for them they could go. The teacher told me the last day that Clara is outstandingly intelligent. "You have to send her to school. It is a sin not to send her." We will have to see. This winter she was at the minister's on a visit a whole month. They have an organ and she learned to play it. She learned a lot of songs and she had to try everything—accordion, violin and mouth organ. She tried to learn to play them as much as possible. Yes, it was interesting evenings when they came home. Then it was to look over the worst arithmetic problems. Lars, Cecelia, and Clara—those three were in the same lesson in dividing so they helped each other.

Lars took the accordion and played the songs they had learned that day, and the rest sang. They are good at learning to sing. Clara can stand up in school and sing a song alone. "Clara

------

[21]*Store* Ole Nilsen was in Bemidji, MN.

sings so everyone has to cry," said Bertha Nestegaard the last day of school. Yes, we should have an organ, and then there would be music.

Yes, now I have written, excuse me if I have written too much, but I think it is interesting for Grandfather to hear about them. They can see how it gladdens me, and I think you would be the same. So everything is well with us—everybody is healthy.

Now my little letter will end for today and I send my loving greetings to you all—first and last to you, dear Father.

Your Sigrid

Selma sends greetings to Grandfather

35 — LETTER FROM SIGRID

Sarnia
November 2, 1902

Dearest Father,

My thoughts have more than ever been with you. The reason is—yes, it is heavy laden to have to say it, but I have to say it anyway. Yesterday, November 1, was our dear, dear Lars buried. Oh, but if we could have had you here the last days of his life. We talked about you often as I sat by his bed, and always it is my comfort when I know you always have me and mine included in your prayers. Yes, Father, this parting is terrible, although it is wonderful to have a good hope that he was saved, which we must thank God for very much.

If you could only have been here and prayed with him and

for him to our God. We did a little, but entirely too little for my heartfelt sorrow. His death didn't come unexpectedly on us either, but as long as there is life there is hope, you know, and that was the case with us. We tried the doctor until the last day he lived. The doctor came and delivered him from suffering and pain, which was great, but not a word of complaining did we hear. In truth, he was patient in his suffering, and hoped himself he would be well again. At least that is what he said to us, but I understood that his thoughts were somewhere else, yes, God be praised he had a peaceful death. Quiet and peaceful was also his whole life.

He was the kindest of our children, and we had nothing to complain about to this time. Lars was conscious until last Thursday, the 28th of October. Right after dinner, we all stood around his bed and he said farewell to us all. He thanked us for what we had done for him. Then he folded his hands on his breast and asked his father to give the Lord's Prayer. When he had said it, Lars opened his eyes and said, "Amen." The three youngest children were at school. "You must greet them, and Uncle also." Yes, father, in the blink of an eye we feel our power is not worth anything. Oh, how much I would have done differently, but now we are separated for awhile. But will surely meet again is His word.

To us all he was always of few words, but well liked by everyone he knew. As he was leaving us, he lay quietly with folded hands, and we talked about God and the Savior, prayed the Lord's Prayer again and other prayers. The time went quietly as he had no pain, he said, but was so sweaty his clothes were wet. 4 o'clock the doctor came again and examined him, gave him his last regular medicine for the night, said good night and left. People came to see him, and he talked to them until 10 o'clock. Lars Skjervem said, "It isn't good for you now, Lars." "Oh, it goes," was his answer. We thought, he doesn't complain, as he lay mostly with his eyes closed. He asked for a drink two times. A little past 11 o'clock his breathing became slower and slower and, with his eyes shut, his hands were folded in Death.

More about his sickness and funeral. Middle of July he became sick, and the doctor said it was the beginning of typhoid fever. So Micheal followed him to Grand Forks to the hospital, where he was for five weeks. Anna was there that time and worked, so visited him every day. They both came home September 3, and then he was weak and poorly, but improved a little at a time.[22] After a month he became worse again, so he went to the doctor who told him the fever was back again, and October 5 the doctor told him to go to bed and he was there three weeks. At that time the doctor came nine times. We spared on neither doctor nor medicine, but it did not help him live, but it eased the pain a little, and he never complained. He always waited for the doctor and hoped he would make him well again.

Our minister was here one time and read and prayed for him and us, and now we need it worse than him. The coffin and clothes were bought for him in town and cost $30. Many people came to the funeral. There were so many people half of them didn't get in the house. So the real funeral was held in the church and it was full. 32 riding outfits followed him. Neighbors and friends covered his coffin with flowers and some expensive wreaths earlier. But the first wreath was given by our poorest neighbor. I accepted it with tears. It was not from an oversupply of money they gave, but the heart, and it was an expensive wreath, too. Margit Lofthus was the one who dressed Lars and laid him in the coffin. It was my second one that she had hidden

---

[22] The family told this story about Lars' homecoming. When Anna and Lars returned home, the youngest siblings peppered him with questions about hospital life. Lars, who had a quiet, studious nature, answered, "Wait until the rest of the family comes so I only have to tell it once."

in a coffin. Who will be next? Both of them are lucky, which we surely believe. Margit bids me greet you. We talked about having you there for the person to give a tribute.

Maybe you want to hear a little about the rest of us also. We have our health, but are struggling with threshing. There is quite a bit of flax left unthreshed. Micheal and one more bought a threshing machine this fall. It was a used one. They got it for half price, namely, $1,000. They will pay $500 this fall. Then they have threshed for the one they bought it from. The threshing bill was $600. Threshing is expensive, you see. We have to pay $200 for our threshing, Knut paid over $100, too. You see, here people have gotten a lot of grain. We got over 3,000 bushel in all and our crop was badly hurt by hail in July. Anna and Caroline Jallo are cooks with Micheal's threshing rig. They each get a dollar a day, a man with a team is up to five dollars a day, so it is expensive to be a thresher, too. It is getting cold now, so they are glad they have only three jobs left.

Knut now has finished his house and is happy. C. Theodore Nelson has stayed with him since harvest and maybe will be with him this winter. He has been with Micheal's machine the entire fall. He is a big strong man and a good worker.

I have recently received a letter from you for which I thank you for writing again. I was waiting till Lars would be well again. We thank God that he was so tired and got to rest in the arms of our Savior. So, live well, Father, and send us a letter. You are all lovingly greeted from me and mine who have now shed many tears.

Live well—that is my wish.

Sigrid

Here come three small girls to you. Do you recognize them?

Sarnia, N.D.
December 14, 1902

Mr. Lars Gjeldaker

Dear Grandfather:

You complained about your stranger girls because they didn't talk to you, so, therefore, I thought I should write to you so you could hear from us.

We are all well and have our health, so then time goes by real fast, so now we soon will have Christmas again.

We have had a very good winter with a lot of nice weather and almost no snow, so it has been a good chance for the children to go to school because we are going to English school the whole winter, but it is only the youngest who can go.

I haven't gotten to go this winter, and I think that is too bad because I am so interested to go to school. We have song school here in the winter for older ones and I get to go to that. The English schoolteacher's name is Clara Sando, daughter of Pastor Ole Sando, whom you probably know. She is very good, and is very interested in the school. She bought an organ herself which she has in the schoolhouse, so it is a good chance to learn to sing when she plays.

Tonight we are also going there. Anna, Micheal and I are practicing Christmas songs, which we will sing at the Christmas Tree, which will be in the church one of the Christmas afternoons. She also has Sunday School every Sunday where she teaches the children Norwegian, so now Clara, Theodore, Nels and Sigvald are there.

I don't have much to write about, so I will break off my simple writing for this time with a loving greeting from me,

Cecelia Lillehaugen

Merry Christmas and a Happy New Year I wish everybody.

C.B.L.

37 — LETTER FROM CLARA AND ANNA

Dear Grandfather,

Mamma says I too should write a few words to you, so I will write a little bit on Cecelia's paper. I don't have much to write about except about school. I am now reading in the seventh book. We like our teacher very much. She has an organ in the schoolhouse, and she also teaches us to play that. We think it is fun. We are now learning pieces for Christmas, which we will present at the Christmas Tree. Sundays we have Sunday School. There are many children. Then we read in the Testament and memorize the Forklaring, Bible History and learn psalm verses. I better quit my writing with loving greeting

from Clara Andrea

Merry Christmas and Happy New Year I wish you all—

Anna

Sarnia
December 15, 1902

Dear Father!

Even though it isn't long ago since I sent you a letter and am waiting to hear, I will send you a few lines again because it is soon Christmas, and a little letter will be pastime for you. I can tell you we are living well and all are healthy so that is good. So if the tears run it is not because of sorrow but of missing Lars. We have to thank God and go by His will. It is a big empty place around here after Lars left, but we will meet again as he said to us. Yes, that strife is over and we will receive a blessing. Although it was a sorrow but then a big joy.

It will be a little sad now at Christmas when we all gather and his room is empty. It is sort of depressing this winter, it seems more or less like we all feel we're missing him. The young are happy now for Christmas. They are as before but for the rest of us our gathering will be more somber this time.

Now that the girls write to you, and earlier you had a visit from an American for Christmas, I won't write any more now for this time. You can visit and ask Mr. Knut, who is coming to visit you.

Then it was a little about the money you ask about. It will be best to send the money to me instead of the others. If I am to have some, will you send $20. Then I will give what is left over to brother Ole for a wedding present because there are several things he will need when he settles down in his own abode.

So I will quit this letter and wish that these lines find you in the best of prosperity and health—both old and young. It is good mother got help from that new woman. I hope to hear all is well from them. I think it is good to have help. I have 3–4 girls and everyone does something. Live well and I hope God will give you a Merry Christmas and a good and blessed New Year. That is wished from me and mine to you.

Sigri

39 ⌒ LETTER FROM SIGRID

Sarnia
February 21, 1903

Dear Father,

Now I have had the satisfaction of reading a letter from you for which you are heartily thanked. Earlier I got the letter with money from you for which I say thanks. Here we are living as before, everyone is healthy now and then the time goes fast. We have had a nice winter so far. The children get to school every day. This month we have had C. Theodore Nelson here with us so they can drive when it is cold.

This winter we have such an intelligent teacher so we are all so satisfied. She teaches them Norwegian on Sundays for those who can learn easily. For the others it is too much. Second day after Christmas there was a Christmas tree in the church and the children read and sang. And we were very surprised when we heard what they had learned. I thought of you, Father, if you could have seen and heard our children how good they were. I know you would have been happy with us, and we thank God for all the good we have received from Him. The children send grandfather the pieces they gave if you can read it. Selma also had one but she cannot write hers, and Clara had more because she is first in school both in Norwegian and English. You should have seen. It was more than one tearful eye because she read a prayer. Yes, it was a wonderful time. Our small children read and the older sang. Someone said about Micheal that he should be "klokker" for his good voice, and now they learn so much in winter as long as the teacher is here, but if everybody doesn't meet up there will be no song, because there are six here to go together—two Nelsons are with, Anna is also home in the winter. She just goes over to the neighbors to help sew off and on. It is so good to have everyone home.

So now we have gotten a little Lars again. That is the name. He was born January 8, and he was baptized the 21st at home and I held him myself for baptism. The minister was around anyway, so he wanted to baptize him then so we didn't have to drive with him in winter when it is cold so long. The boy is healthy. He is long and thin, but quiet and good, and of course he has to be that when he is Lars.

This is becoming a mixed up letter you get now so I better quit. The small boys think that grandfather will write just as nice letters to them as the girls. It is a novelty to see your hand-writing, which is just as nice as ever, and now I think you are old. Live well, you dear, and greet all who would like to hear from us. We hope to hear that all is well with you again.

Your Sigrid

[1903]

Greetings from the distant Norway to Sissel Birgit Lillehaugen from the 75-year-old grandfather.

Receive my New Year's wishes. It gives me so much joy to see that everything is going so well with you all over there in the Hills, and to note that you are already so good at writing and are seeking for more knowledge and enlightenment.

I should like to remind you of one of the parables, which tells of the entrusted talents. Our Lord has given you many talents to direct. You are born of Christian parents, in a Christian land, where there is rich opportunity to exercise reverence and virtue. Your parents He has put in a position so that they have the means to help develop your intelligence. You have teachers, men and women, who plant and water, and, finally, there are the five talents. You have been endowed with good abilities. With all these pounds (talents) you are to bargain so that when He comes requiring an account, you will be able to say, "Lord, you gave me five pounds, and with them I have gained five more."

Dear daughter of my daughter, there are some children who are so thoughtless, that when they are a little above the others in the class in knowledge, they look down upon them as though it were due to their own diligence. They will not acknowledge that it is the Lord's work and that we have to give an account. Significant are His words at the end when He says, "... be faithful over a few things, and I will make thee ruler over many things. Enter thou into the joy of the Lord." This promise of the Lord is confirmed literally in every age. When you have been good and obedient so that your parents and siblings praise you and you see your parents' and teachers' happiness, then you enter into the Father's joy. Still more important—when our hour comes when we shall harvest what we have sowed, then in truth we shall go on in to our Father's joy.

Now you saw how good brother Lars had it although he was in pain. He went into his Father's joy even while he was here. Yes, also you who with him had a share in that joy, for you had good hope about his life after this one, where you will be with him again.

It is a wonderful profitable thing to commune with God daily in prayer. And when you then talk with Him about your affairs, then also tell Him that you have a grandfather and grandmother in Norway who greatly need His help, for they are old and weak and totter like a reed in the wind.

I commit you to the almighty God.

Your own Grandfather,
Lars Gjeldaker

41 ✒ LETTER FROM CECELIA

[1903]

Dear Grandfather

I should write to you and thank you for the nice letter, but that will have to be later now after all the others have written, but I had to write down Sigvald's verse for him. I greet you from Uncle. He is well and we see him almost every day.

Friendliest greetings from
Cecelia Lillehaugen

The Piece Sigvald had Christmas Eve

1

Julen er kommen
Det lyder saa södt
Budskabet lyder en frelser er födt
Lyset nu straaler
Fra himmelen herned
Nu kan hvert hjerte
Faa glade og fred.

2

Glad deg I Jesus
Og favn ham o skjal
Da har du gaven
Som ret gjor deg sol
Vandre i lyset
Og folg ham blöt tro
Da skal du hisset
Med engle faa bo.

3

Med dig kommer mindet om svunden tid
I hjemmet blandt vore kjere
Da glemmer helt let om vor dagelige slid
Da synge vi dig til aere
At os er idag en Frelser födt.

4

Gid, altid for os det var Juletid langt
Lettere vi fandt

Glaeden bleve störe og sindet saa blid
Naar ret til det haab vi os bandt
At os er idag en Frelser födt.

1

Christmas is come
It sounds so sweet
The message sound—a Savior is born
The light is now shining
From heaven down here
Now can each heart
Get gladness and peace.

2

Be happy in Jesus
And embrace him, oh soul
Then you have the gift
That will make you blessed
Walk in the light
And follow him with tender trust
Then you shall be raised
With angels to live.

3

With you comes the memory of past times
In homes among our loved ones
Then we forget entirely our daily struggle
Then we sing to you with honor
That to us today is a Savior born.

4

Oh, that for us it would always be
Christmastime for a lighter time
The gladness will be greater
When we are tied to that hope
That to us today is a Savior born.

Sigvald, 7 years old

42 ⟋ LETTER FROM THEODORE

Dear Grandfather,

This is what I read at the Christmas Tree Fest this winter.
Friendly greetings from me.

Theodore T. Lillehaugen, 11 years old

1

Saa kom du igjen du deilige Jul
Med fred til de bamle og unge
Med glade til hver dei vil höre dit bud
Og synge med lydelig tunge
I dag da blev meg en frelser född.

2

En takk for dit möde hvert eneste aar
Thi du har kun gladden i fölge
Du bringer til hjertet os deilig vaar
Med dig kommer haabet's Bölge
At os er idag en frelser född.

1

So you come again you beautiful Christmas
With peace to the old and the young
With gladness to each one who will hear his bidding
And sing with loud voice or tongue
Today for me was a Savior born.

2

A thanks for your meeting every single year
Because you have the gladness to follow
You bring to our hearts a daily spring
With you comes hope's wave
That for us today a Savior is born.

43 ⌁ LETTER FROM NELS

Dear Grandfather,

Even if I'm young and poor a man to write and I have to write with my left hand, I hope you will excuse me if you would be so kind. Mamma wants me to write the piece I gave by heart at the Christmas Tree Fest. You can see how I write. It is not good so now I better quit and send a friendly greeting from the little

Nels T. Lillehaugen, 9 years old

De engle smaa fra himmel hjem
De sang saa smukt og södt
Om lidet barn i Bethlehem
Som julenat var födt.
De sang om fred og glede stor og velbehag hos Gud

Som Jesus bragte til vor jord, O glade Julebud.
De priste Gud for kjarlighed som var saa sterk og stor
Sin egen sön han sendte ned som barn ja som vor bror
O Jesus er vor egen bror, O glade, glade stor
O prise Gud al folk paa jord med glade Jubilkor.

The angels small from the heavenly home
They sang so beautiful and sweet
About the little child in Bethlehem
Who Christmas night was born.
They sang of peace and gladness great and of God's pleasure
That Jesus brought to our earth, O happy Christmas words.
They praised God for love that was so strong and great
His only son he sent down as a child, yes as our brother.
Oh gladness, gladness great
Praise God all folk on earth with glad Jubilee.

44 — LETTER FROM CLARA

Dear Grandfather,

I will now write you a letter to thank you so much for the nice letter I received awhile ago.

I have written the piece I gave at the Christmas Tree for you. Maybe it could be of interest to you to see, the young boys have written theirs, too, if you can read it. Maybe it won't be very easy to do. I haven't anything to write about that would interest you, so I better quit. I would like to get a letter again if you have time and it isn't too expensive.

From Clara Andrea, 13 years old

Greet Grandmother and Uncle Nels and Ole, but most of all you are greeted from me.

1

Nu har vi puntet vort Juletrae
Se stjernen I toppen blinker
Nys stod det bart under vinteren's sne
Nu det med frugter vinker.

2

Ind under grennene snart du ser
Hvad vi har skjult saa lenge
Deiligste gave dog Jesus er
Aide du ham ei stenge.

3

Sneen har dekket de blomster smaa
Marken er hvid derude
Tusinde stjerner paa himmelen staa
Vinker til os ad rude.

4

Snart skal vi Vandre i ringen om
Tanken mod himmelen iler
Synge om barnet som til os kom
Deilig det mod os smiler.

5

Södeste Jesus velkommen ver
Under var nod hernede
Stjernen over din krybbe ser
Deiligste Juleglade.

6

Ah, er du kommen saa lang en vei
Börnene smaa at favne
Saa du saa fattig paa straa for meg
Da skal du meg ei savne.

7

Kunde du meg fra din himmel se?
Endag jeg er saa ringe
Vilde du krone og arv meg gi
Evige liv at bringe?

8

Var der ei engle der oppe nok
Sangt over sol og stjerne?
Vilde du mig i din hvide flok
Finde igjen saa gjerne?

9

Var ikke himmelen's harpe klang
Mer end nok for dit öre?
Vilde ogsaa min lille sang
Evig i himmelen høre?

10

Ja, du har elsket hver barnelil
Kjobt dem i evig eie
Gjerne du bare as alle vil
Hjem over örken veie.

11

Saa vil vi ile til krybben hen
Give til dig vort hjerte
Södeste himmelske börneven
Takk for din bitre smerte.

12

Takk at du hviled i krybbens skjul
Takk at du os vil farne.
Maate vi hisset i himmelens jul
Ingen af os dog savne.

1

Now we have decorated our Christmas tree
See the star on top blinking
Lately it stood bare under winter's snow
Now with it fruit laden winking.

2

Under the branches soon you see
What we have covered so long
The greatest gift, however, is Jesus
Do not lock him out.

3

The snow has covered the small flowers
The ground is white out there
Thousand stars in the heavens stand
Wink to us out there.

4

Soon we will wander in the ring
Thoughts hurry toward heaven
Sing about the child who to us came
Beautiful at us they smile.

5

Sweetest Jesus welcome be
Under our need down here
Stars over your crib see
Beautiful Christmas gladness.

6

Oh, have you come so long a way
Small children to embrace
You looked poor on the straw for me
Then you shall not miss me.

7

Could you see me from heaven?
Even though I am so small
Did you want to give me a crown and inheritance
Everlasting life to bring?

8

Was there an angel up there
Saint over sun and stars?
Did you wish me in your white flock
Find again so willingly?

9

Wasn't heaven's harp clang
More than enough for your ear?
Did my little song also
Forever in heaven hear?

10

Yes, you have loved every little child
Bought them in forever ownership
Willingly you will carry us all
Home over the desert way.

11

So we will hurry to the crib there
Give to you our heart
Sweetest heavenly children's friend
Thanks for your bitter pain.

12

Thanks that you rested in the crib's shelter
Thanks that you us will embrace.
May we be raised in heaven's Christmas
None of us shall be missing.

[1903][23]

My dear Sigvald,

I suppose you would like to get a little letter from your Grandpa who is so old and lives in the Old Country. It will have to be now, or there would never be a Grandpa letter because soon there will not be any more Grandpa in the old country. You may not be able to read yet, but you will soon learn to read it and then you can write a letter to me.

I am sending you a little knife so you can practice making toys for your little brother Lars. You may not yet realize that he sees you as his big hero, and you are not the little boy any more. You will have to have patience with him and thank Jesus for giving you another Lars in place of the old one He took home to be with Himself. He paid you in cash because you sang so nice for Him by the Christmas tree.

Now, Sigvald, you will likely want to give Him *something*. I can tell you He would really like to receive something from you. He has said, "My son, give me your heart." Giving Him your heart means to obey Him and be kind, never tell lies or cheat, never be dishonest or disobedient. But be diligent, proper, sincere and obedient from a sincere heart, not out of duty or to be noticed or to be paid. That is how you give Jesus your heart, and He will repay a hundred times more. Who knows, maybe Jesus will want you to tend His lambs. He needs many shepherds because He has so many lambs. He said so. Pray the Lord of the harvest that

---

[23]Note by Sigvald on 4-6-79: This was written in 1902 or 1903 by my Grandfather Lars Gjeldaker.

He will send out workers in His field. This is a command from Almighty God.

> *Sing while you have your youth*
> *in your bright summer*
> *The shield of your song goes to the heart*
> *and returns to your heart.*
> *Some day when you are not so glad*
> *These songs will return to you,*
> *These songs will return to you.*

46 — LETTER FROM SIGRID

Sarnia,
April 25, 1903

Dear Father!

I suppose it is time for me to answer your letter that the stranger boys brought to us. I have never gotten such a big Norway letter before, so now I have to give you my heartiest thank you for everything—not the least for the young boys. They became so excited and happy—as children can be. They wanted to write and thank you right away and thank Grandfather for the present. So now I better do it for them this time, and they can write later themselves. It was good for them to be remembered as well as us.

Your dear letters always have such good words, prayers and encouraging words, which can serve us well. Yes, Father, many thanks for everything. There was one who became offended and thought she was forgotten, and that was Selma—no knife from

Grandfather. Then the tears really came. I told her that she had not written to you. Then it was to find pen and paper. The letter was soon finished and papa had to find an envelope. When it was in the mailbox she was happy. I asked her how long she thought she would have to wait and she said for sure three days! Now all is well. Nels is going to hide his knife until they butcher. Sigvald read the letter through the first evening, but he had to spell every other word, I think. Theodore thinks Grandfather is an incomparable man to write, and I think the same. Many people are surprised when they read Nels' letter.

Here it is spring now. The boys began late in the field. They have seeded some wheat. Micheal is a great person to work. Then it will be Uncle Knut later, and Knut is so afraid for his horses. The newcomers have hired out to the neighbors for $20 a month. They are so bashful and backwards, it's hard to get them to come in and eat. We were company at their place and had goat prim Gro had made. It's been a long time since I have tasted her food. I got a picture of Gro. She is so young and pretty. Will you give her my hearty thank you for the same? I also got from brother Ole and family. Such handsome people. It makes me happy that you speak well of her. It is good for them and for you who will be living together.

They are going to begin seeding again. Yes, I think it is nice with a small farm where expenses are accordingly and as long as there is no shelter there. Large family, but when it gets to be so many to clothe and feed it is good to have more in the hand or it will be as it has always been to work for others.

There are so many examples of that, all the land around here is taken. Those who want Homestead land have to go to Minot or to Canada. There are people here who are moving away because they haven't watched out for debts, so they are selling their quarters here and getting free land again. Here the land is up to two, yes even $3,000 a quarter. That is a lot of money. The poor can never pay that price when they buy. Nelsen now wants $2,000 for his farm.

I promised to tell you what I bought for my money. We took them and added to it and we sent after a $50 organ. It is now here and is diligently used by all except Lars and me. We haven't tried it yet. It is a pretty thing and the last thing I own after grandmother. Everybody wants to learn to play and Clara is the one who can show the rest. It is so funny the smallest can teach Micheal, Anna, and Celia. Everyone has to obey her. Yes, "Clara is an intelligent girl in everything," said the teacher. It is all she will be, but I think something else and that is she could soon be called home because Lars called, "Clara" about two hours before he fell asleep.

Clara Sando was so well satisfied with Clara in school and she let Clara play the organ every free time, and taught her lessons that others would have paid 50 cents for each lesson, and she got these instructions free "because there is no one as intelligent as Clara." Those are the teacher's words. We are thankful that it is easy for them to learn and have a chance to do so. We are going to send her to school this winter, they say. We will have to see. Now she has it nice. She is at her uncle's, Knut L. Nelson, and cooks for him when he is in the field. He will give her one dollar a week and then she is at home after dinner every day, and plays the organ and teaches others, but she takes it so sensibly. She does not become proud over it.

This is getting too much, maybe. Micheal says I should greet you and say thank you for the knife. He'll probably come one day himself walking to you and then you can visit. They will possibly go together—both Lars and Micheal. Then they can say themselves that is one year since these pictures were taken so you can see how they looked then. It would be fun for us if you could look in on us. I think that would make you happy. It is so touching to me when Clara plays and the others are curled around the organ and sing. There is one I think is so touching. It is one that says, "God Be With You Till We Meet Again." And this one: I will write the first verse, so maybe you have heard it before, but it is so pretty when it is sung:

> *O lyse minder,*
> *Fra min Barndom's glade tid I tanken rinder,*
> *O saa sod og blid*
> *Dog det Bringer smerte,*
> *Naar mit blik tilbake gaar,*
> *Ofte stakels Hjerte, Du nu lide faar.*
> *Fader O Fader*
> *Ofte tanken gaar til dig,*
> *Fader O Fader*
> *Glem, O glem mig ei.*

> *Light thoughts from my childhood happiness come*
> *Sweet and pleasant, although it brings pain*
> *When I look back. My heart now must listen.*
> *Father, O Father, often thoughts go to you.*
> *Father, O Father, do not forget me.*

So you see this is like the thoughts I sing. Now I better quit these lines with the wish we could meet with God. Live well, then, and everybody there at home be greeted from us all here.

From Sigri

C. Theodore Nelson is not with us now. He has hired out to a neighbor for a month.

Sarnia
May, 1904
Pentecost Day

Dear Father,

You are often in my thoughts so I will see if I can get a letter you can read. Yes, now it's Pentecost time and the beautiful, delightful green ground and trees newly clothed in celebration with this beautiful weather. Rain and sunshine make everything grow and the eye can see beautiful fields and meadows. Praise be to God for everything outside and inside and that we can all be healthy and can work—both old and young.

We have now had a lot of work because we have built our barn. It is large and expensive. Tosten has here what he has paid. It is $3,600. If that is all I don't know. Just to the carpenters it was $200. We had four carpenters one month because they painted, too, at the same time. Now it is in use for the horses. You should see it. It is 66 feet long, almost as wide with a lot of hay room, and shed on one side for hay because we put up 100 ton. There are plank floors in the horse and cattle rooms.

Then there is also a fork to pick up the hay from the load and that takes two horses. It takes the load and makes it easy to unload. There are 16 windows, and in the west end there is a well so cattle can get water inside during winter. I hope you some time get a picture. The carpenters took pictures when they were done, but they were ruined, so we will have to try another time. I would have to have you see our home on paper when you don't come and visit us. I am well satisfied and thank God for everything good.

The next chapter will be about the children. Anna left the 26th of April to Minnesota to visit her Uncle Lars and is still there.[24] Cecelia has been with me this spring and works for two—a big, strong, ruddy-faced girl almost like myself when I was on Gjeldok. She works, never complains but just carries on. Clara was in Michigan until June 2nd. Then school was over this spring. She is intelligent, well liked at school. Her friends and teachers are encouraging her to continue with school. She is also studying reading and organ playing. Now she is home, takes part in all work. She has this winter boarded with the same people as Helge Hoff so we are well acquainted with him. He is a musician. Plays the organ, violin and guitar. He rented an organ and bought a music book so Clara should have a chance to learn, and it did help her. Hoff is often here. He says he saw his Grandmother Helga one time and now that he sees me it reminds him that we are alike. So I guess I have gotten old. Oh, yes, I have good health, but I don't like to work much now. I have good girls so I can get out of a little work now.

It is Lars that should have good health as long as he can't walk by himself. But he is good now in a walker like you made your small boys. Tosten has made one now for Lars, so with time maybe he too will be able to walk. I hope so. He is intelligent and sensible which is good. Micheal and Theodore finished seeding so Micheal went on a trip west to his homestead,[25] and Theodore began Norwegian school, which we were so lucky to start. Yes, Nels, Sigvald and Selma are all going. We were so lucky to get a teacher—a daughter of Tollef O. Sando from Iowa.[26] She has been together with Sven now three summers and taught Norwegian. She is very intelligent. I was there one day and visited them. It was

---

[24] Lars Lillehaugen, brother of Tosten, lived near Hayfield, MN. This is where Tosten, Sigrid, and their three children lived when they first arrived from Norway. In later years, Lars and his family moved to Benedict, ND.

[25] In western North Dakota.

[26] Helene Sando, who later married Micheal Lillehaugen.

good to listen to them. She has about 20 pupils but has been used to teaching, and has had twice as many children.

Yesterday, the 13th, we were to Ladies Aid. There I talked to Sidsel Hoff. She has gotten old and just as fat. From west here I heard that Michael K. Mehus[27] is sick and that they have no hope that he will live. Yes, we all have time to wander around but we then have to be prepared to follow when tidings come. It is strange for people to wander so unconcerned for their salvation.

So, I suppose you want to hear about the Knuts. They live well. One works inside and the other outside, so they have it nice. Knut farms more land than his own, so he hired Knut G. for the whole summer. Ole Bjella is so wonderfully well liked where he works—no one can compare, according to Ole.

Soon I will wait for a long letter from you so I won't tire you any longer with this reading now, but quit with as hearty greetings as this letter can bring to you all—old and young. Live well and pray for me and mine.

Your Sigri

48 ⟶ LETTER FROM SIGRID

Sarnia
November 20, 1904

Dear Father!

It surely is too long between each letter now, but it is your fault because I wrote last. I have often thought of writing, but

---

[27]Michael Mehus lived at Brinsmade, ND.

then it gets postponed again. Yes, thank God we are all well. That is the first happy thing I want to say to you, because we are all well and each one struggling over his own.

This fall we got a good crop around here. Micheal was out and threshed and the girls were along and cooked. When threshing was over, Micheal went west to his land to live until Christmas, and proved his Homestead. Johan Espegaard is with him. Knut Gjeldager went too and met Engebret Mykinghaugen and they went to search for land. Anna and Cecelia went west to visit relatives in Brinsmade, and to Myking and Helling. They will be gone about two weeks.

Clara was confirmed October 30. She was praised very much by her minister. She got a Bible for a confirmation present. She has now gone to Michigan City to go to English School. She takes four music lessons there. She is smart, said Ringstad. The minister, too, asks her to come to Petersburg every meeting to play the organ. We don't know if she has the courage. Theodore has begun now to go to Norwegian School, which is being held by a girl at a farm four miles from here. We have Nels, Sigvald and Selma at English School two miles from here.

Then it is Lars. I have to write about him. He is big and fat but will not learn to walk. He sits on the floor and lies down and rolls over on his back and rolls from one room to the other. I guess he's so weak in his feet so he doesn't like to stand and walk. The English nurse said I have to begin bathing him. He is soon two years but is about like he is one year. He is beginning to say mama and for the first time this summer he got teeth. He is an Askepot[28] in every way. I suppose he'll get as well as he should anyway even if it goes slowly.

---

[28] *Askepot* means someone who stays at home and works hard, a "Cinderella." Sigrid realized that little Lars would never be able to leave home and live on his own. Because of his limitations, he would be a "stay-at-home."

This summer they laid the foundation for our new church and it was a good meeting. Mrs. Helling visited us here and also Nels Svensen and family. This week we had a visit from Even Nelsen and Lars E. Helling. Ole Bjella stays at brother Knut, also Knut E. home. We thought Knut would go home this fall, but no, he has to take care of his horses and cows, dog and cat, and he doesn't want to be away that long.

Randi Jallo asked me to send you a greeting and tell you she was satisfied how you divided the money, but there are two others. If you will give each one dollar so they could buy a little keepsake from her for Christmas. The two she thought were Borgil Holto and Birgit Søndre. Then there was a message if you would send her a few lines back. Her address is: Mrs. K Jallo, North PO—Walsh Co., N. Dak. She would like to hear how they are living. She begs to excuse her for the bother she is making for you, and hopes the gifts will come for Christmas. Yes, she likes to do good to others. She has not forgotten the conditions in Norway for the "working class."

How are you living now? I suppose you are pensioned now[29] and have a new room added. I hope you are satisfied. If a person is satisfied, it doesn't take much to live well. For my part, I think I have it good. Many have it worse. I have house and home and daily bread. What else does man need? Sometimes other things come which we wish wouldn't be that way, but man can't expect only sunshine here in the world. Me and mine have a lot to thank God for, I think. I try to remember this, and try to teach the children the same. It is to teach them in their heart so it will bring fruit. With this big flock, the Lord has helped so far. Our children have the good Word both from home and away. However, there are many to teach in this world and many people to learn from.

---

[29]Lars Gjeldaker received a pension of 550 *kroner* (approximately $61).

We are now writing November 21 and it is such nice weather. On Friday it was many that plowed. It has been only the milk cows we have had in at night and given hay to. The others are living well out on the prairie. This summer we built another room so this winter we will have it nice. We bought a new stove that burns both night and day and doesn't go out. We have enough coal. But, you understand, we paid $45 for it. This spring we are going to build a new barn. This fall the threshers were here one day and a fourth, so we had to pay $250. It is expensive to thresh here, you see. Many farmers have paid $500-$600 and more. Yes, you are probably tired of reading this, so I will quit and send my heartiest greetings to you and all who wish to be greeted.

Greetings from Sigri

49 — LETTER FROM SIGRID

April 1907

Dear Father and rest of the relatives,

I have received your welcome letter awhile ago. You are so heartily thanked. I see you have been visited by sorrow and separation. Yes, everybody has to have the trial of that kind. Then it is to pray for help to bear it with patience as it was for you. The old can experience trials as they come, but it will be a lonesome time for the poor parents. Their only little beautiful boy, their daily comfort and happiness.[30]

---

[30] Sigrid's brother Nels and wife Birgit lost a son, Lars. He was born January 17, 1905 and died February 5, 1907.

They all have our sympathy in their sorrow. I know from experience how it is to lose one of our loved ones. One cannot see the good before later, and we open our eyes to all dangers and temptations there are for us and our loved ones in this world. Many times my thanks rise to God for the ones who are gone. I often wish to be in their place, free, saved and happy forever, and meet our loved ones, as Lars said to us, that we will all meet him again there.

Brother, do you remember when I wished you better luck with your Lars than we had with ours? Yes, see, now would you wish him back again? Never! It is heavy to find ourselves like this, but we have to bow under God's will. I hope to hear your little Birgit is all well again. It must be a hard time for you all, that which will long be remembered.

Here we are living as usual. We are all well and we are struggling with snowstorms yet and it looks like it will be a late spring. Often people have seeded a whole lot by this time and now we have big snowdrifts. So now we are waiting for spring. Knut is living well. Micheal S. Lillehaugen is there. The only thing he lacks is a housekeeper. You better send a nice, kind girl over to him with Sigri. I suppose she has visited you so you have heard about Sarnia. Now it is another Nelson here, namely, Theodore Nelson. Now there are four here. He has bought a farm here.[31] Now I must quit with loving greetings to you all from us here in Haugi. I wish you to live well.

Sigri

---

[31] Christopher Theodore Nelson bought a farm from Tom Berve, who left the area.

October 23, 1909

To the Dear Ones at Home:

Thank you for the letter with information about Father's homecoming. Lucky for him who has struggled, and who now we believe has moved to a better place. Loss is now great for you who have had him among you all the time. It will be a big empty space, I can think. But I suppose you were tired from the care you gave. It would have been good to have been home among you even for a week. There are now many questions I would like to ask you, but probably they won't be answered anyway. I beg you please write to me about his last days and time of death.

It didn't come unexpectedly either for him or for you. They are lucky who can die on the daybed and not be jerked away in unexpected death. If I could only have laid a memorial wreath on his dear bier. I hope he won't be forgotten there at home among the relatives and friends. Yes, now he is well hidden, even if he is not forgotten. We have now survived and we should follow his footprints and live so we can find again an end to strife. But to gain this we have to champion against sin and everything evil, as it says in the song: "We have to pray and suffer but there is a day when there is gladness, and we soon will get to move Home." You have probably already received Knut's and my letter and seen our decision that as survivors we divide everything in a brotherly fashion, and not trouble and strife which often happens.

We hope, then, that you will avoid all unpleasantness with dividing the inheritance, and so you both honor it satisfactorily. If, at some time, you have the chance, could you send me something of his remaining things as a last remembrance of Father—that would be good.

So a few words to you, Mother, who now sit alone again. It must be lonesome, I would think, to lose your partner after so many years of following through life. You are so lucky to have your own room and your own to look after you if you need something, and you get to have Bibi—grandmother's girl. That is a comfort and pastime. Now you can get rested out and look back to life's sorrows and joys and changes. I would finally wish you could write a letter once in awhile. It will be so lonesome without Father's regular letters. You better be so kind and not forget us. Let us hear once in awhile from that dear home in Ål.

Thank Nels for the picture of the pretty little Lars. He is very pretty. What was wrong with Bibi, was she timid? Knut also has a pretty boy, so like himself, but he isn't Lars though.[32] Yes, here we live well. We had an unusually good year in every way—very much grain—I can't begin to tell how much. Live well, all of you, and let us hear about Father's funeral.

All be greeted from us in Haugi.

Sigri

---

[32]Lionel Norman Nelson was born June 18, 1909 to Knut and Amanda Schenstad Nelson. Had he been born in Norway, he would have been named Lars, after his paternal grandfather.

Sarnia
November 23, 1913

Dear Mother!

It's been a long time now since I heard from you, but today Knut came with a letter from you and one from Nels. Then I got a greeting from you. Thanks for that and that you haven't forgotten us. It is so seldom we hear I sometimes think you don't care to hear from us any more, but now I found out that isn't so. I'll send a few lines so you can hear from us again. We are living well and have good health, so that is the best of all good gifts we daily get from God's hand, and there are big benefits we daily accept from God's hand and that is a great benefit.

Everyone is well here except Helene, Micheal's wife, who this past year has been sick and under doctor's hand for healing. Only God knows how long a time she has left. It is hard to live with a spouse who is sick, and so hard to forgive everything and follow Jesus, and do what He asks. She is living in hope that she will get to live with her loved ones. It is hard for a mother to leave her young ones. The young are also so kind. The first part of October they went to Iowa to her parents to be with them this winter because it is a milder winter there than here. She also needed a hired girl, and it is so hard to hire someone who is good. There is a grown sister and a good and understanding mother, who is best of all when something has to be done. Micheal and Tollef stayed here until November 17. Then they went too. Micheal hired a boy to take care of chores this winter. The house stands empty, and when and where they will be back again is a big question.

I think it so strange when the family gets spread so far apart. Here now this winter it will be lonesome. We are used to having everybody around at Christmas, and now Micheal and family are in Iowa, Sigvald goes to high school in Fergus Falls, Minnesota, Clara is in Washington and teaches in a big school in a big town.[33] There are five school buildings there and 56 teachers. The first day of school 970 children were registered, and many more have started since then so there is a lot to take care of there, but she likes it. She is along in the choir and Sunday School so she has a lot of work, she says. She gets $80 a month. It is good pay, but board and room has to be taken from that, and it is very expensive. It is very beautiful there. There is no snow or cold weather in winter—just rain instead of snowstorm, so it is nice to live there.

Where Sigvald is, there are only a little over 200, he says. People ask him what he wants to be. They ask if it is a pastor. He hasn't decided that yet, but he wants to go to more school, and Theo and Nels are home so he does not have to work at home this winter. Up to this time, we have no snow or cold weather— bare ground and nice so it is easy to take care of animals this winter: 18 colts, 21 horses, 4 pigs and 15 sheep.

Today is Thanksgiving Day, 27th, and we have been company to brother Knut. We had a lot of good food. It would take too long to name everything, but there was lutefisk and lefse, and that was the best of all, I thought. Everyone was there, Iver and Anna and Almeda; Theodore and Cecelia and Aleda. Amanda's sister has been here for awhile, but she wants to leave again now. They have it good and nice up there. Everybody was well, and it was nice to visit them.

---

[33] Wenatchee, WA

I stayed over one night at Ole Bjella this week and took care of their little boy, Lars. He has pneumonia, so it is now the third time he has had this sickness, so maybe he can get well again this time, too. He is very sick, poor thing.

Even Nelsen lost a six-year-old boy of the same sickness. They had six children, and now there are only two left. They have been married eight years this month. Another neighbor has been married two years and have now gotten their third child, and she was 18 [on] August 15.

Now Tosten is going to the barn to milk. We have two new cows to milk and one old one. In the morning we milk four. Then I am alone. Selma goes to school this winter and is now 16 years. She didn't go this fall because she was along and cooked for the threshers. Since then she was with Micheal when Helene was gone. He had to have someone and Selma was able to help. I can do my work most of the time.

Now I have written so much, you are tired of reading it.

Greetings
Sigri

I would like to see all of you this summer. Greet your letter writer and Gro. I suppose she is just as healthy. Greet the brothers and their families from us all here.

September 12, 1915

Dear Mother!

I wish I could look in on you and see how cozy you have it now. Thanks for the good letter. Greet Birgit and thank her for the sympathy I received from her.[34] When I got your letter, I felt like writing again, but it has been postponed again until now. I must send them a card later. We and ours are all well and have had a cozy summer. At Knut's they are living well, although Knut has a bad back so he cannot lift anything heavy, and had to have a hired man steady, and it is hard on the money, $35–$40 is the pay for men there now. He is getting such a good crop and he has only these three children.

Are you getting new neighbors? How does Gro like it? I should also have written to Ole, but now I am sending two cards, one to each brother, and they can take whichever they want. Ask Ole if he got five crowns this spring that I sent to his Sigri in the letter I sent to Birgit Rimeslaaten. I registered the letter to her in April, and I haven't heard from anyone if it has been received. Be so kind and let me know if they have received it. The Post Department is responsible, and I have to investigate from here. I got ten crowns from Knut K. and put in the letter. Now you must live well and be heartily greeted from

Sigri

Be so kind as to get Birgit to write a letter to me again.

---

[34]Nels Lillehaugen died on February 3, 1915.

1916

Dear Mother and Siblings,

Days and weeks have turned to months since you have heard from us. I have often thought about writing, but it is postponed. I must now thank you for your dear letter, Birgit. Thanks for sympathy and sharing our sorrow. It is so good to get sympathy from our dear ones. We got many a good sympathy letter, but the loss is just as deep. I feel it every single day yet, and now especially working around the threshing machine. He had been with them five falls, the last one as engineer. Now Micheal will have to help without him.

Now we have lived a beautiful summer again. It was chilly at first and a lot of rain. It looked like it was going to be too much rain for the lowland. Here we got the right amount of rain, and everything grew and became a crowning year of everything except corn. That needs warmer weather, so it won't get ripe this year. It will begin to be long, cold nights. September 3 Micheal began with the threshing machine here. Threshed three days and threshed 4,000 bushels of grain, and we still have several days of threshing. They have to thresh one or two days at each place, so now they have one quarter at Knut and one at his. In the morning he will move to John Espegaard. Theodore is along and hauls water. Sig hauls grain from the machine, and Selma is along and cooks for the fourth year. She has to get up early, and there are 18-20 men to cook for. Breakfast 5 o'clock, Dinner 12, Lunch 4, supper evening meal after 8 o'clock. It is after 10 before they can go to bed. It is two of them—an older girl who has cooked three falls for Micheal. He says he misses Nels so because he was always along. He will be missed all places—inside and outside. I have shed many a tear these months since he left us. In my memory I see him healthy and strong. The home without him is "empty" inside and outside, but I have the hope he has it good, and thank God, because it was His will and He wanted him that time—to take him home, and then he is freed from troubles and the world's problems which are lived daily and contended over and over again. We have now put up a nice tombstone over his grave like we put on the others. It cost $75. It is blue and white marble. Now there are three Lillehaugen tombstones—Lars, Knut and now Nels.[35] Big, strong men, but it doesn't help. Sigvald, Knut Lillehaugen's son, was confirmed in August. The Sunday he had communion his mother went with him. Ole wants to get rich, he ran two binders all day.

This summer I had thought I would go to Wheelock to Anna Helling and all I knew out west, but in July when I could go then Anna went to Canada to her sister Birgit who lives there.

A little more about threshing in North Dakota. The boys were home on Sunday and they said they had threshed over 300 acres in six days and over 10,000 bushel grain. They have left 1,700 acres to thresh this fall, so they need a lot of sunshine.

Clara came home again and in July she taught Norwegian School. Now it is September. She began teaching English School in Whitman for nine months, a long time. She stays at Micheal's and drives every morning and evening. She has four miles to drive, so you see we are very alone now during threshing. It is easy for me to make food for us two, but is often full house at the table. In harvest we had two hired men. One was Tosten S. Lillehaugen. However, here at home many come and want to stop and have food and room. Then there come agents and tramps. No one is turned away—food or room. As company this

---

[35]Lars and Nels, sons of Sigrid; Knut S. Lillehaugen, nephew of Tosten.

summer we had visits from Sigri Svensen and Mrs. Planting or Aagot Bergi as she calls herself. Guri is with them in town.

Knut[36] is on his farm with his renter. Then he can muddle around all he wants to himself. But then he got company from Minnesota.

Tosten was to a Hallinglag and there he met Helge Ellingsgaard and Mrs. Peterson. They came here—both of them. He has been a minister in the same congregation 32 years, but then he had a stroke and had to quit, but his son is pastor so they can stay with him in his home. They liked it so well up here. So we are going to take a trip to them after threshing, I think. Our neighbors are all well now and also well at our place. Margit Lofthus lay very sick this spring for awhile but now she is well. She had a stroke and became almost speechless with it. Their daughter Ronaug died in August after several years of lying sick in bed.

Since I started this letter Mrs. Lofthus has had a heart attack so only God knows how it will go.

54 ⁓ LETTER FROM SIGRID

September 13

Margit Lofthus is very sick.

---

[36] This Knut was the father of Aagot Planting.

Brocket, N.D.
October 16, 1917

Dear Mother,

Today I received your loving letter of August 7. I am sending
you my loving thank you for the same. I see you have me and
mine in your thoughts and memory. I am so ashamed that I
haven't written to you, and I beg forgiveness that I have waited
so long before you hear—but sometimes I think they don't care
to hear from me because it takes so long to answer my letters.
But as it is with an old loving mother who never forgets her
children, but has them in loving memory night and day, over
to us according to what you say in your letter I will then send
you a letter. Mother, I hope it finds you and all the rest of the
relatives in best of prosperity, and I can say the same from here
about us all.

We are living in a critical time here in free America, and God
only knows what will become of this with might against might,
and sorrow and loss for people. Expensive time and unpleasantness. What does all this mean—does it come from God? Or is it
the authorities' fault? These enlightenments and questions are
unanswered.

I hear Knut has written and told you all the news so I won't
muddle about that. They are all living well and that is good. So
Ole has another son. Greet them. I would like to see them all. I
suppose they are big and beautiful children? Nels will be only
two so there isn't much help, but look at us who once had 11,
and now we have only Theodore left at home. The two youngest
just went to school. Selma, who was supposed to be my help, was
gone eight months last fall, and will be there that long this year

too, if we all get to keep our health. This summer she taught 1½ months of Norwegian School. She had over 20 children and was well liked, but she wants to be an English Teacher, too. She also teaches music—piano playing, etc. Sigvald was also home this summer but has now gone back to school. It takes so much time and money there.

Today we had snow for the first time this fall, but then I suppose it will thaw again.

56 ⤙ LETTER FROM SIGRID

Brocket, N.D.
October 17, 1917

You stated that you are somewhat good with your health. How good it is that God is so wonderful, but I suppose the time is coming also for you. That time does not give me any pleasure. I often think about what Grandmother said that no one should get old—yes, they have their troubles in the past and we have ours again. "O God in Christ's blood make my farewell time good." Yes, that is what we all should pray. I have it always good, always healthy and do my work, which is often quite a bit. But then it is so good to have something to do. I therefore thank God every day. Many have to suffer pain in many ways for months. Tosten hasn't been so good lately, so this spring he went to the doctor and then there was an operation. He stood it well and was gone three weeks, and came home well and healthy. He has been very well since, but you can see he is not young any more. He was 70 years this spring, but it is good when one can seek a doctor and get help, which they can do in many cases.

So I hear Gro has had a misfortune. Poor thing—it must have been painful. I suppose they also have a struggle about Knut.[37] I think, probably, that if Knut only wasn't where he is—those poor people that are sent to war. The last we heard about him was in June. Then Engebret Haugen went to him and he said that Knut was quiet and kind and talked sensibly, and was just like he always has been. He had asked others about him and they said he was always kind and capable—but he had the same thoughts—namely, that he had done so many terrible things, etc.

Yes, we all thought it was so troublesome to hear about Knut. He was so well liked by people here. God uses suffering to benefit us people by having us have afterthoughts about this so it will make us make use of our time to do everything for our everlasting well being. We are now living in a strange time with strife and enmity instead of peace. There is discord and dissension affecting people and land.

This summer we have had a cozy time. No storms to scare us or take our crop, which was mediocre, and certain places it was too little rain, so it wasn't too much, but it is a good price for everything we have to sell. At the same time, what we have to buy is the same price, too. We read in the paper that it is the same there at home. For example, we sold two fall sheep for $10 apiece, two pigs we got $100.65 for because they were one year old. Cattle at this time are $50-$60—yes, even up to $80 apiece. So the ones who have them to sell, it's good, but those who have to buy to live on—yes, that's a different story.

So, mother, you will get a paper I am sending you. Let me know if you got it next time you write. If you like to read it, I will gladly send you another one. Remember that, then.

---

[37] This Knut is unknown today.

I hope Nels will now find time to write to me or to Knut. Then it will be the same as we read each other's letters.

Last August I was on a trip to Minnesota to Helga Ellingsgaard. A lady and I were at a big fest on Sunday, and guess who we saw there. It was old Asle Kortgaarden and his son, Levor. I went and greeted him and said who I was. He looked and looked at me, but he couldn't remember me. I knew him well when I had looked at him. This summer we were also to a Hallinglag and there we met many people we haven't seen since we left Norway, and it was so wonderful to meet them again after all these years. Halvor Varaberg, Asle T. Rimehaugen, Erik O. Sundre, two sons of Myre boys, two sons of Oleiv Tveito, three cousins of Syver Roiseplas, etc.

I suppose this is of no interest to you. You would rather hear about ours. They are all well and Micheal was married again last March. So now both he and his children have it nice and good. This summer Micheal built a big and nice barn that cost a lot over $2,000. His wife's name is Maria,[38] a kind and nice wife.

So we will be satisfied if these lines get to you. You are much greeted and thanked for your dear letter.

Greet all relatives and your good letter writer and family are heartily greeted from me and mine.

With best wishes for time and eternity.

Your
Sigri

---

[8]Marie Moe

October 18, 1917

A few words to you while we are waiting for Tosten. I want to talk a little bit and tell you that last week we cooked milk prim two times—for Anna one time and one for myself. We are milking only four cows now and in the summer eight, because we let two calves suck, and they are nice and big.

I thought maybe you would like to hear what children went to Norwegian School for Selma this summer. Anna's Almeda; Lionel, Beatha from Knut's; Micheal's were Tollef, Hilma, Sylvia; also Selvin Espegaard; from Ole Bjella, Lars, Hilda; from Knut Lillehaugen, Gena, Selma; Mabel Sandelien; Luella, Myrtle, Olea Lofthus; Norris, Esther from Even Gudmundsrud; Sadie, Alma, Lorin from Halgrim Skjervem. These were the Hallings, but there were more children.

Clara begins now in winter as an English teacher. This summer she was far west and taught Norwegian School. She likes herself well but she always finds friends wherever she goes, and wants to make it nice for those who are to learn. She is praised a lot and much sought after as teacher in both languages, and that is needed, as there are many unruly children and unconcerned parents—especially relating to religion. It is such a mixed blending of nations many places in this land.

You knew Johanes Espegard. He died last winter and left his wife and five children, and two old parents, but they have their daughter, Turi, here, so they will be taken care of. Then it isn't so bad. They were also good people.

Live well everybody.

Sigri

Does it take as long for my letter to get there as it takes for yours? Yours was opened in England.

58 ⌒ LETTER FROM SIGRID

February 13, 1919

Dear Mother!

I just received your dear letter written December 7 on February 5. So I here send you my loving thanks. The letters get old now and it had been opened. How long are they going to continue that when the war is over? Oh, how wonderful it is that the war is over. I hear in your letter, mother, that your health is good. Oh, good it is for you and for Nels and his small boys that you are well. You were on the seter this fall. I suppose that was a lot for your age.

So you also have had a visit from the Spanish Illness. Here in this land it has been bad and the fall's deaths have been great. Many empty rooms as after those who have been called home. Here at home there is a big, empty room after our dear Theodore—who died November 16. He was then 27 years old. Theodore is missed and grieved by us all, but it is our hope and belief that what can better happen than to travel toward his God. He was so kind, and worked at home in his place. He was always at home and never went around recklessly. He was always satisfied and never caused us any grief. Now he is gone but never forgotten, and we trust that after his hard time he has it good with God and that He has his soul's mercy. His illness was short—not quite a week. He was very sick the last night, but he was conscious to the end. He bade everybody farewell and hoped to come to God and that we'd all meet there.

Yes, I hope we all can meet for Jesus' sake. There is a comfort in sorrow and loss to have the hope that they have it well, as our pastor said last Sunday: "To all of you who have lost someone of your loved ones, remember that they are now saved and free and shine like the sun in the Father's kingdom. We have to be happy and thank our God that he has planned it so good for us sinning people. We must thank Him for all the good for body and soul that we get daily."

Now all of them are well again. But it was a bad time this fall when Knut Helling became ill first when he worked here. When he became better our hired man, Torger, and Theodore became sick and we called the doctor to see them. Then Theodore got pneumonia and that is what he died of.

Sigvald was still in the Navy and got home only three days for the funeral, which was November 20. At that time large crowds were forbidden because schools, church and other gatherings were closed up several weeks on account of contagion, but the illness raced to all places anyway. Middle of December the illness broke out again in all places. Entire families became ill and many died—parents of children and vice versa. One family had four sons. All four were married and three of them died. So there were three young widows and 13 fatherless children. One of the widows is Turi Lofthus, daughter to Sander and Margit Bjella Lofthus. Mrs. Halgrim Skjervem died and there were seven motherless children, etc. It was much sorrow and loss. I suppose it is God's purpose to wake up people to think, and in that way he will use many kinds of methods. God willing it is for the best.

Now Sig has come home and we hope it is for all time. It is our purpose now to keep him on the farm because we were so lucky to have him. There are lonely homes again—some crippled, some in their caskets, and most of them are resting on the French ground. When Sig went we were sorrowing for him.

Theodore promised us at home that there was no danger for him—but see what happened, we had to get used to him being gone and do the best we could. We stand ready when the Guest who we call Death comes. Oh, if we then could meet him. It was strange about Theo. About two weeks before he became sick, we heard about two boys who had died. He sat and thought awhile and said, "If that sickness comes here and I get it, that will be the end of me." Another time he said about the same thing. After the last conversation, he took care of his business. Sig should have his land and all his horses. Tollef should have his watch. The rest he gave to his brothers and sisters and they should divide as friends. He had quite a bit of money and he gave it to several. He had a nice funeral, nice casket. It cost $147. There were so many that needed caskets, so they became so expensive, and here they buy them ready made, caskets, clothes, flowers and everything.

It is almost evening, so I will have to say good night. All our children are now well except Clara. She has not regained her health since she was sick. All of them at Cecelia and Micheal were sick, too. The only one who didn't get the flu was Selma, and she was two weeks at Micheal and took care of them. The doctor was out there four times. But they became better again, thank God. As I said, everybody became well except Clara. She is not strong so she is home. Both the girls took schools this fall in Wheelock.

Selma went west and began school 13 January after two months vacation because of the influenza epidemic. Selma boards at Anna Helling. Engebret O. Hougen is also there. Last week Guri Myking died. We have not heard the cause of her death. The last years she had been living with poor health and many troubles.

Christmas holidays were not the same this year as other years, because we always used to have all our children and grandchildren home for Christmas Eve. We had a Christmas Tree and we tried to build up each other the best we could. This year there was not a single one home and those that lived around here were sick. So each one had to stay in his own home. The children complained and said it would be no Christmas if they couldn't get to grandmother's at Christmas. It was odd, however, because Anna Dokk came here with the mail that day and Knut Helling was here so I got them to sit around the Christmas table. Christmas Day we all got to go to Knut's.

We have had only one church service since September 18. Then it was a funeral for a boy who died away and was brought home in his casket. Yes, it has been an odd time these last years. May God bless us for time and eternity. I think it is God's purpose in this.

I can greet you from Knut, everything is well with them all. So live well all relatives. Loving greetings first and last to you, dear old mother, who is gradually heading to the grave God gives us after our wandering. We will gladly meet up there.

Sigri

59 ⟶ LETTER FROM SIGRID

Sunday, November 23, 1919

Dear Mother and Brothers!

Now it has gone weeks and months since we have heard from you. I hope all is well with you all just as it is with us and our children and other relatives. Good health is now here among us so we are very thankful, because last fall we got to see and go through something else. It was good, however, to learn to appreciate good health when we have it. Grief after the loss of those who have gone before us is with us daily, but with thanks for what they were to us while we had them with us. With me, especially, I feel when they are gone I appreciate when I had them with me.

In regard to the weather, we now have bare ground, but 9th and 10th of November we had a big snowstorm, so we have had poor roads to this time. Summer was nice, although July and August it was very warm and dry. So the grain was light (it was just like they said in Norway—then the food turned white). So that's the way it is here—a lot of light wheat. The rye was better and also the barley.

So I have some news to tell you. On 11th of November our Clara was married to a Norwegian pastor, Rev. J. A. O. Wulfsberg of Michigan, N. Dak. She will then be only 14 miles from home so we will see her often. They are now on a wedding trip but will be home after December 1. Clara had taught many to read. She taught English School 11 years—nine months each year and often one or two months Norwegian. She had one month free each year. Last winter she received $95 per month. Those are the largest wages she has ever received. For Norwegian School in the summer, she was paid $60 per month. So that was good pay, but board and room has to be subtracted from that during winter.

Selma has now begun her second winter teaching 80 miles away at a German Settlement. She has 17 children in the school. There are two Norwegians and all the rest are German. She boards with some German people and it goes fine, she says. She has nine months and $85 a month. Then it goes off $20 for food and housing. We have only one left at home of the whole flock and that is Sig. He is our milkmaid and farms our land along with his. He has this winter Tosten S. Lillehaugen with him.

They are two good milkmaids, and they have over 20 horses, over 30 cattle, 22 sheep and 2 pigs.

Now I must quit for today because Amanda[39] called me and invited me to come there for dinner, and I would like to go because they always have such good food. Knut has a good home, a very nice wife, and big and intelligent children. I should greet you from them and Knut said he will write soon.

As far as our children, Micheal and Cecelia are all well. They have both bought new pianos with money they inherited from Theodore. All six got $450 each and they wanted to have a remembrance from him.

Our neighbors came here one evening before Clara left. It was 20 of her school children she had had last summer. They bought a pretty dish of silver and gave her. It cost over $12. Other relatives were also along. It was about 40 people here throughout the evening. They brought cakes and cookies. I cooked coffee and we had a cozy evening together. Last Thursday our Ladies Aid met at Cecelia's and there were many of us. The pastor and his wife were here also. Now next Thursday will be Thanksgiving, a holiday which has been ordered by the President to have Thanksgiving church services with offering to Missions.

Now it is the 20th of November our good hired man left. He was on his fourth year. We will miss Torger Aardal. He wanted to go to Norway to his father and mother who are both living yet. He talked about taking a trip on the *Bergensbanen*[40] through Hallingdal, and we asked him to stop at the Ål Station, and look you up just to greet you, and H. Helling from his children here, namely, Anna and Knut. They were both here. So when Torger comes to you, be kind to him who was one of ours and a

---

[39]Amanda Schenstad Nelson, her sister-in-law.
[40]Train

nice boy. What he tells you, you can believe. I told him to take a photo of Mother, the small boys and the house and you, Nels, hold your horse. I can greet you from Aagot, Mrs. Planting. Her health is better and her father is the same. She has the youngest girl of Aagot Holtto. Hans has the other six himself.

Knut and Herbrand are married now. Knut Helling has rented a farm now. He bought three horses and cows, etc. He is a good boy. Anna worked at Lars Gudmundsrud last summer for awhile. There was also Ole Ulshagen and Nels Vangen around there where Lars was. Here the paper is ended. Good night. Live well everybody.

My letter has to close with loving greetings to you all and wish you all Happy and Blessed Christmas fest and a long letter back. You, Nels, are usually good to write when you want to.

Sigri

60 — LETTER FROM SIGRID

January 28, 1920

Dear Mother!

Ever since I got your dear letter, which I thank you for, I have wanted to write to you so you would get it for your birthday which will be next month. Mine will be tomorrow and then I will be 64. Think, so old! This last year my hair has begun to turn a light gray. Yes, time has its way. Is it now you will be 80? If we could have, we would have come now and visited you. We would then take along good food, and you would cook coffee and we would be what we in America call a "god teim" good time. We do here, too. The old see their friends and talk to the poor old things who sit alone and check on them. They cannot get anywhere, not even church, which would be such a morale builder for them all. You complain about your chest, but you can see and hear well yet, I have it excellent to always be healthy. I see and hear well. I sew, crochet and spin. Now these days I have been spinning, and I am making yarn for many others. I have knitted mittens and socks for the twins.[41] They got new stockings for Christmas and for everyone at Micheal's. I also knit eight pairs of mittens for our Ladies Aid. First I give them the thread and binding. I am about the only one around here who spins and have wool, so I have to be ambitious, then. This fall I sold over 200 pounds wool. I have spun on my good old Trageton spinning wheel. It goes around as fast as when I sat on Gjeldok and spun and sang to the spinning wheel's tempo. I think back to that time so often. I dreamed one night that I was on my way home to Norway and think—I was as close to home as north of Sundre. I saw Gjeldaker over the hills but I didn't get to come home to Mother even if I was so near. Would you have been glad to see me there again?

I have it good now. Only two men to cook for and I don't go out and milk in the winter either. We work for the missions now. We do not have many members but we are good workers and there are so many around the world who need help. They asked for help this fall for French children so clothes and money were sent. Now we have to help again where the war ruined things. We are now living in a strange world but we have heard that before—we have heard enough of so much unrest, strife and accidents.

---

[41]Clara and Clifford, children of Knut and Amanda Nelson

January 30, 1920

Here I will have to continue this letter. I can greet you and say we are all well to this date. That is good after having a tough winter so far, but those who have a good house and plenty of hay for the cattle, and a windmill to pump water, and water in the barn as we have now, it is good. Theodore made everything so handy the last spring he lived—and so was he ready, too—all his work is now handy for Sigvald, but he has had too much education to be satisfied on the farm. There are other things he was interested in because he could have been a teacher in high schools with big pay and lighter work. God rules so we don't really know what is best for the youth's future. We have to turn them over to God's hand. "They, not I, shall rule."

It is soon February 1 when Nels left us well and the 5th came home in a casket. That is a memory I will never forget. I can never hear Song 220 in Landstad hymnbook, whether at home or away, without seeing Nels standing before me the last evening he was here at home. He and other brothers and sisters stood around the organ and sang that song. He had such a nice tenor voice. With God's gracious help his soul is freed because God does not want any sinner to die.

So I wish you everything good and everlasting. Live well, greet my brothers.

Your Sigri

August 1920

Dear Mother!

You are often in my thoughts so I want to write a little line to you again! Thank you for your loving letter I now received. I see you were entirely alone at home. I should have been there with you then and you wouldn't have been lonesome for awhile. Oh, how enjoyable that would be to meet, but I guess we better give up that hope in this life—if we can only gather happily together with our loved ones—old and young.

It is fall here again, and it was so cold last night that the potato grass froze a little. That was pretty early. We have had a nice summer with nice weather so the crop is average. Today Micheal began threshing. Selma is cooking for the threshers again. So now I am alone with the work. She has been home since June.

We two old ones took a little time off and were in Fargo to the Hallinglag this year. There we met so many old friends and it was so nice. I met Lars T. Bjella and Margit. She asked about you and when we parted she said, "You must greet your Mother." We talked about Beihovd, etc. She is thinking of taking a trip to Hallingdal, she says. I saw Botolf Hefte there and Asle Haugo, Halvor Varaberg and three children of Sven Noss, etc. I can't name them all here.

Rather I'll tell you about this summer, we have gotten two little girls in our family. Mrs. Micheal had a girl 21st of June and Anna Helling has been there this summer. The 29th of June Cecelia had a little girl. They were both baptized July 25. The first one's name was Edith Theodora, the other was Valborg Lillian. I held her at baptism. Then the little one became sick for a week and had many hurts. She was released from here on Friday the

13th and was buried the 15th of August, Sunday afternoon. You see sorrow and happiness wander to hope. We have another sign that death is a hard struggle. May God help us through everything so we can be saved and be freed from the strife and trouble here.

One day someone stopped in an automobile in front of our door. When I came out there, there were Mr. and Mrs. Planting. "God dag," Aagot called, "now I am coming from Beihovd." She then picked up some beautiful fish. They had taken a trip to Minnesota where Herbrand now lives, and there are so many fishing places there. So we had fish for dinner for everybody that day. So you see we can meet and have it cozy here, too, especially after these good autos have come in use.

Selma drives our automobile wherever we want to go when Sig is too busy. Aagot's health is improved after she had an operation. Her father lives alone out on his farm. He is a little better, not so mean, she says.

You must greet E. O. Hougen if you see him, tell him we are busy here.

63 ⌒ LETTER FROM SIGRID

August 15, 1920

Farvel Sang

I

Syng som Nu bor ei Synden mere
Nu er da tiden kommen
At jeg til graven gaar.

Jeg venter kun paa rummet
Jeg blandt de döde faar
Jeg var vel Eder Kjar
Den stund jeg var i liv
Men i maa mig bort give
Jeg er ei lenger her.

2

Farvel, I Foraldre kjare
Og söstre ligesaa
Nu sorger i og grade
Mens jeg saa let som dinne
Skal svinge mig til Gud
Der i stor Aere side.
Og jeg ei mere skal lide
Nogen slags smerte nu.

Digtet av Lars Gjeldaker 50 aar siden

Farewell Song

1

Sing as now sin doesn't live any more
Now the time has come
That I am going to the grave.
I am waiting for the room
I will get among the dead
I suppose I was your loved one
The time I was alive
But you must give me away
I am no longer here.

2

Farewell, you parents dear
And sisters the same
Now you are sorrowing and crying
While I'm as light as down
Will swing myself to God
There with great honor shall sit.
And I no more will suffer
Any kind of pains now.

Written by Lars Gjeldaker 50 years ago

Now the 19th of August I had Ladies Aid meeting here and so many people came. Think, three pastors were here, our Ringstad with family, Olsen, our neighbor pastor, and Clara and her pastor. It was over 50. We served coffee, sandwiches, cake, cookies and pickles. For the lunch we took in $8, we are working for missions. We are glad for what we can do to help because there are so many heathen in the world. This summer, 3rd and 4th of July we had a mission meeting. We had a pastor here who had been in China seven years. He is going back again this fall. Sunday we had offering for missions. We got over $100, but what is that when they need money for the millions of heathen's souls who need to be won over to Jesus. Wonderful it is to serve God—wonderful for men and for women.

From Sigri

Good morning the 23 August

Here I have to write a little bit about Knut who is so poor to write. They are living well to date. It is not really a problem as long as grandmother is with them. I don't know how long that will be. It is a lot to do for her, especially clothes washing. Now for awhile, Selma has been there one day a week to help. Knut had two men again during haying and harvest. Now they are gone so it is only themselves. But next month it is school again for the three oldest. They are intelligent children and Knut is a kind father to them. It is such a good thing there—they have a beautiful home also. Then it is to pray for them to have their health. Then it will go all right even if the sorrow is heavy.[42]

Here is the end of the paper so this will be the end of this conversation.

Live well and loving greetings to yourself and your intelligent letter writer and brothers.

Sigri

Hymn sung at little Valborg Lillian Nelson's funeral August 15

I

Et alvors bud fra Evigheden
Os Herren sente til vort gavn
Og hented hjem til Himmelferden
Et barn, han lagde i vor Favn

---

[42]Amanda Schenstad Nelson died on February 14, 1920.

Nu er det löst fra synd og Nöd
Og nyder Himmelhvilen söd.

2

Thi lad os ikke mere grade
For den som Gud herfra utreiv
Men lade os fra hjertet bede
At de somend tilbage blev
Ei falder maa i Synden's Garn
Som fanget har saa mangt et barn.

3

O Herre, gjor os alle rede ved
Sand Omvendelse og tro;
Hjelp vaage og at bede
Til striden skiptes om til ro!
O gjor du os for Kristi Död
Vor siste Afskeds time söd.

Landstad 697

I

An earnest command from eternity
The Lord sent as His gift
And called home to Heaven's peace
A child, he laid in our embrace
Now is released from sin and need
Enjoys the Heavenly rest so sweet.

2

So let us not cry any more
For the one whom God took away from here
But let us from our heart pray
That those that are left behind
May not fall in sin's entangles
Which has imprisoned many a child.

3

O, Lord, make us all ready with
Pure conversion and faith
Help us to venture and pray
Until the strife turns around to rest.
And for Christ's death make for us
Our last farewell time sweet.

65 ⟶ LETTER FROM SIGRID

December 29, 1920

Dear Mother,

Now that we have Christmas and my thoughts and memories are there with you at home, I will take my pen and send you our greetings, although I think you have by now had a visit by Americans who have brought you greetings and our picture. So you will hear from us. But now at Christmas I received a big and delicious Christmas present from Mother and sister-in-law. It was with great thanks I now daily get to taste the good

Gjetost.[43] It is so good, and many want to taste a little bit of that Norwegian cheese, those like Knut Helling and Pastor O. Nilsen.[44] He was here during Christmas holidays because he is our pastor this winter. It was so wonderful we could have him with us Christmas Eve, that is, our family and Knut's. There were 11 adults and 13 children at the table. After we had eaten on Christmas Eve, we had a Christmas tree with a program by the children that were here. The pastor gave a sermon so we all had it cozy and good. Uncle said he had never had any Christmas that he had been with so many relatives, and it was so wonderful for us all. I always think of father when I see and hear that man. He is beginning to get gray now, but is so nimble in his actions and an extremely good speaker. He held service in our church second day Christmas. Afterwards he went home with Micheal and stayed overnight.

Yes, our Christmas has been cozy so we have much to thank God for, and we have been healthy all that time, and enjoyed life with our children around us. I believe you have heard from Knut so I will just send greetings from him that everything is well there. Tuesday we were up there and we were guests.

It has been good and nice weather to this time. People drove their automobiles way till Christmas, so we have it nice in every way. Now at Christmas I got so many gifts, cards and letters. Among them a letter from Mrs. Anna K. Helling. She went to Washington[45] this fall to her brother Ole and her mother's sister, Sidsel Hoff. She lives where he is and is a widow with only one daughter. She is well-to-do.

There is no news about anyone you know—only that one of

---

[43] Goat cheese
[44] Sigrid's uncle, Reverend Ole Nilsen
[45] Puyallup, WA

our neighbor boys[46] went away at Christmas time to get married and will be home for the New Year and there will be a wedding celebration they say. Knut Helling has gotten work. Anna Dok, who this fall had an operation, is getting better but it took a long time for her. All our children are well, and now this winter we have only Sigvald at home. One now out of eleven. That isn't many but it's less work for me. Now I have such a good time to read, for Christmas I received a big, good book from Clara and Selma, I was very happy with it. My job is mostly knitting. I gave away ten pairs of mittens for Christmas but many of them were small.

So you must have a thousand thanks for the cheese—both you and Kari. Live wonderfully well. I wish that for you.

Sigri

Greet everyone who calls me aunt, and also others who ask about us. I mustn't forget Mrs. Söberseter either.

66 — LETTER FROM SIGRID

December 1, 1921

Dear Mother,

I have thought so much about you lately wondering why no one has written to me for Christmas. Last Sunday I was up to Knut. There I got to see a letter from Brother Ole—but not a word about Mother was in there, not even a greeting to me. I have to reach the conclusion that me and mine are written

---

[46] Lester Skjervem married Amanda Johnson at Elbow Lake, MN.

down in your "forgotten book" at your place at home. That is not so with me. I remember all of you dearly, not you alone, but relatives and dear old friends, the district and the white church down in the valley. Everything is so auspicious in my memory of Ål and is greater when it gets closer to Christmas. Ole thanked brother for the picture that Lars G. had brought him. Didn't I send all of you pictures with Mrs. Erik Haakenson last fall for Christmas? Hasn't she brought them to you??? It would be fun to hear if she didn't bring them to you.

I want to tell you, old Mother, that at Knut's they are living well and all of them are healthy. Grandmother left them last October, so now he has to cook, bake, wash and iron. He does everything real well just like many women. The three oldest go to school every day. The twins are big and pretty children. They are along outside when the others are at school.

Now Christmas is over and I want to tell you how cozy we had it. There were church services first, and then we invited our children and grandchildren for dinner. Also Knut with his five. Micheal has six now. The youngest was born November 13. His name is Carl Arnold. Anna has one girl, Cecelia has three girls—when we count the youngest, we had 29 for dinner. After dinner we had a Christmas tree, a little reading and song. The children read pieces they were going to read the next day in church. First we had services and afterwards the Christmas tree. We had such a wonderful time together. The children were so good both in song and declamation. There were 36 children in the Christmas tree program. The youngest wasn't four years old yet. She sang two verses of a song alone and she did real well. Manvel, who will be four years on January 5 gave the first verse of *Thy Little Ones, Dear Lord Are We*.

The third day we gathered at Cecelia's and now Friday at Micheal's. They have built a new big house. Our house is old, and so are we, so that goes together.

This winter none of our children are home—just two boys that rent land here and I board them, so we are four, you might say. Selma is now home over the holidays. She teaches school in a town four miles away. The weather has been so nice this time that we have driven the auto until Christmas. Christmas day we drove to church in the automobile, but now we have gotten a little snow so now it will be the sleigh.

As you see we are well to date and also neighbors you know are well. Do you remember Knut Jallo? He died this fall. Must quit now and greet all you relatives and your young ones. Thank your letter writer so heartily from me and also his wife—also Gro. She has also become old and poorly.

Live well and best wishes for time and eternity.

Sigri

1

Nu er Julen kommen, glade hoitids dag
Mangt et hjerte banker nu av fred og vel behag
Over sine gaver alle er saa glad
Men jeg fik en gave vil du vide hva
Best av alle gaver er Jesus,
Det Gud's Lam, som tog min skyld
Ja, al min synd ag skam.

2

Venner's sjone gaver farer ganske kort
Denne gave varer om end Himmel Jord flyr bort
Alt I den jeg eier Helbred Liv og Fred
Glade trost og haab, ja, evig salighed.
Best av alle gaver o.s.v.

1

Now Christmas has come, happy festival day
Many a heart is pounding now with peace and pleasure
Many are so happy over their gifts
But I got a gift, do you want to know
What is the best of all gifts?
Jesus, God's Lamb who took my guilt
Yes, all my sin and shame.

2

The friends' beautiful gifts don't last long
This gift lasts even if Heaven's earth flies away
All in this gift I own good health, life and peace
Happy Comfort and hope, yes, eternal blessedness.
Best of all the gifts etc.

Little Theresse Nelson sang these two verses in church at the
Christmas tree. She will be four years old next May.

67 — LETTER FROM SIGRID

December 15, 1921

Micheal has built himself a big and practical house this summer with all modern heating apparatus, lights and water. He has
electric lights in each room, inside and outside. They now have
six children. The three oldest go to school and the others are
home. I will now give you the names in case you have forgotten
them: Nels Manvel 4 years, Edith Theodora 1½, Carl Arnold was
born November 13 and baptized the 17th. The minister came to

Ladies Aid and they got him to come in and baptize the little one before winter comes. Up to this time we have had only nice weather so people drive daily in their automobiles. We had a nice fall and winter.

Now no one is home—only father and two men to cook for. Selma is teaching in Whitman and this winter Sig is attending St. Olaf College. You see the nest is empty now and the birds have flown, but six of them have gone before to wait for us. Many happy memories about our departed loved ones, especially Clara is deeply missed by us all and her lonesome husband. And the four congregations where she, for a short time, got to work in the Lord's vineyard. Blessed is her memory. She was an unusually good and kind woman. So it is us two. How long a time we have before God takes us to meet everybody at our Lord's where there are many rooms we do not know.

Live well then Mother, and Merry Christmas Wishes.

Sigri

68 — LETTER FROM SIGRID

New Year's Day 1922

Dear Mother,

Will today begin a letter to you. I was so happy when I received your most loving letter. Many thousand thanks. It came to me Christmas Eve when the church clock was ringing in Christmas. Yes, it was so cozy to get your letter, so well written. As I was reading it, I thought Söberseter had written it, and on the last side there was his name. I hear you are somewhat well. It is good to be healthy and we must always love and thank God, therefore, because time goes so fast and we get older. Then we get God's call to fly away from here. Yes, we have had many of ours. Many memories of the ones who have left us and hope they are happy.

Now the last is Clara whom the Lord took home last March 9. She was happily married one year and four months. She had with her in her casket her little one-week-old son who was baptized by her sickbed. When they asked her what his name should be, she said, "Frederick Theodore." "Do you want to call him Theodore?" they asked. "Yes, Theodore and I were always such good friends and I like the name." The other name was the pastor's father's name. Clara did not get to be old. God had a better home prepared for her. I am sending in this letter a write-up in the paper written by O. Nilsen, who was with her the last hours she lived. He gave her Communion and her husband two hours before she left. She smiled and thanked Uncle when it was done and he said, "You are tired now so you better get some rest." I knew then that it would be her last sleep and how that time was grave for us all.

Clara lived quietly and good and tried to live a useful and happy life for all she was with, and a nicer and more beautiful death and funeral was never had. At the funeral the casket was by the flower-decked altar. There was a wreath from relatives and friends around and his four congregations. I cannot write everything to you, but I have it all in my memory about her. The best of all was when O. Nilsen said he was certain she had received a blessed death.

My thoughts often go up where the dear ones have gone and I pray for a happy reunion with them.

Clara now rests beside her four brothers and little sister until Resurrection morning. May God give us the happiness when we all gather together. O God, for Christ's blood make our farewell hour good. There is more to write, but read the piece I'm sending. At the funeral here the casket was taken inside the church and there was more than one pastor. Flowers decorated all over—even the pulpit. Here was where O. Nilsen said he was with her the last hours. In Michigan, he used a text—Be faithful until Death, etc. Here in Sarnia in church the 13th it was Revelation 19:7-9. Find them and read them. Those words have often made me happy, and Uncle said he had used that text only once at a funeral, and we surely had much to thank God for. There are a lot of questions but everything the Lord does is well done.

Printed obituary:

Mrs. Pastor J. A. O. Wulfsberg, Michigan City, ND, died in the Deaconess Hospital in Grand Forks March 9, 1921 and was buried with a few days old son the 13th. Mrs. Wulfsberg was the daughter of Mr. & Mrs. T. M. Lillehaugen and at her death was a little over 31 years old. Her life had been a beautiful example of faithfulness and interest in everything good, including teaching the young people God's word. As teacher and organist, she had from her youth served God's kingdom wherever she was called. At the church services in Michigan City the following pastors took part: Professor E. Hove and Chr. Andersen, both from Minneapolis; Pastor Ole Nilsen, Grand Forks; also Pastor J. Ringstad, who had baptized and confirmed the deceased; Pastor Thomas Anderson, Petersburg, ND.

Burial was from Sarnia Church, where five siblings before had been laid to rest in the family cemetery, and where H. C. Olsen spoke. The dear departed died with a Christian Confession and with full trust in the Savior's grace. The Lord's name be praised.

—O. Nilsen

May 3, 1922

I have been thinking about you so much in the last days, so today I want to write a little bit. First I will greet you and say we are healthy and living well to date. Knut and his were all in church Sunday. They were dressed so nice and Knut is a good house mother. He washes and irons and mends clothes for himself and his children just as well as any mother. The children are also very intelligent so it goes for those who are left alone too. Knut is healthy, too, so that is good. He has a hired man to work in the field so he has the inside work. Sunday we were all to church. Here everyone who has room to ride to church and now that spring is here and everybody drives autos there is room for many.

Sunday our pastor began Sunday school and Selma is one of the teachers. Micheal has three children who go, Knut has three and Cecelia three, it gets to be a lot from here. It is a big help to teach them Norwegian and the Lutheran teachings. Cecelia had her little 5-week-old daughter baptized. Ole Bjella and Gunhild were sponsors because they are such close neighbors. She was named Viola Clarice! She has four nice little girls now—two at school and Theresse 4 years. She had a little one two years ago who died, so she has had five girls. I told her, "Now you have had five girls like I did once, are you going to now have six boys also?" Yes, it is a funny world, we now have no one at home of our whole flock. We have two strangers who farm our land. Sigvald does not like farming. He went back to school again last fall. Selma is teaching school in the closest town and is home for the weekends. Now that we have such nice roads, she comes home each night. You will soon get company. Anna Helling is coming home and you will hear about us and what we are doing. I hope to hear that everything is well with you. Age invades more and more with you, too, and each day we are one step nearer the grave, which is our last rest. There rest all hands—there fade all wreaths.

It is so nice here now. The grass is getting green, the leaves are sprouting—yes, spring is beautiful when everything is growing anew and coming to life. April was raw and cold, so they didn't begin seeding until April 17. They thought it was late but now the wheat is up and the field is getting green. Cows and calves, sheep and lambs can be out. We have 17 big sheep and 17 lambs now but we have three left. So it is my job to shear the sheep.

Now I have come to the last side of paper and don't have much news so I will close with a prayer: I thank God and praise Him happily for awhile because He shows His grace for all time in many ways with prayerful humility. He wants to give grace that we will be eternally in His Heavenly Kingdom. Yes, God, give us all this.

I wouldn't have anything against taking a Norway trip this summer, but it doesn't seem to happen.

So I hope this letter, old mother, will find you well, and that you have it well—a nice, peaceful home and kind people to live with, a room of your own and board. I wish you the best of all God's word for comfort and cheer night and day. Live well and our loving greetings from all of us relatives around here. Greet my brother's family. I got pictures from Nels and his home and horses and sons. Also you. You are not old.

Sigri

September 18, 1922

Dear Mother,

I reread some old letters and I read that you were so glad to get letters from us, so I thought I could make you happy so I will write again. I have the time and the wish to do it.

Today Sigvald went back to his school and Selma, also, has taken a nine-month school in Whitman and the school began also today. Every Sunday there is Norwegian School in our church, where Selma is one of the teachers. She is also organist when needed, once in awhile, when those who have been hired can't be there. She strives to be like sister Clara, but she will never be that good. We have to be happy that she does as well as she does. Many young are only after pleasure and noise.

September is thresher's month here and now it's soon eight weeks since they began their work. Up to this time, however, the weather has been so undependable with rain and cloudy weather, and it is unhandy for the threshers who have to go on with the work in the field. Here we received an abundant crop this year. The summer has been so wonderful. We have had only good weather for everything that needed it. The crop around here is the best we have ever had since we began here, but it is not good for the grain to stand out in the rain. The price is also poor—under $1 per bushel, and that is not enough for those who have to hire help. Everybody has to hire and hired men are expensive. Now it is $5 a day for haulers and much more for the ones who run the machine. So it isn't all pay for the farmer!

I don't suppose this is interesting for you so I'll greet you from Knut and his children. I should tell you they are living well, and yesterday they all got to church with their pretty and clean clothes. The twins were there with the oldest to Sunday School. It was the first time they were there. They were so quiet and pretty. Each child got a card to take home. It's to entice the small to come along. This summer Knut hired only one man, otherwise they have done the work themselves. Selma has helped a little once in awhile with baking and cleaning the place because the girls will be going to school when it begins. Lionel is so grown up now so this fall he is doing a good job threshing for a 13 year old. He is big and strong and Knut gives them everything they need and looks after them—the dear children so they can attend children's school.

I am so glad every Sunday we have church so we can gather in God's house and hear the same good God's Word and our familiar songs—among other songs:

> *O Holy Spirit, enter in,*
> *And in our hearts your work begin,*
> *And make our hearts your dwelling—*
>
> *Sun of the Soul, O Light divine*
> *Around and in us brightly shine,*
> *Your strength in us upwelling.*
> *In your radiance—*
> *Life from heaven*
> *Now is given overflowing*
> *Gift of gifts beyond all knowing.*

"God's Word is a lamp unto our feet and a light unto our path." Yes, just to read the little Catechism is our learning.

September 22, 1922

Now my pen has rested many days but I haven't been resting. Wednesday I was over to a sick old lady who has been in bed
eight years. She has two boys who keep house and take care of
their mother. Thursday I boiled five prim cheese. They weren't
too big because I give away some of them and they are lighter to
carry. Today I took one of them with me to Knut. He lives about
as far from here as to Styrkestad. He took me home again in his
car. Four children rode along. This week we have had beautiful
weather. There is no frost and the ground is full of flowers in the
garden and the lawn is green and nice. Yes, we certainly have it
nice, thank goodness. But many have it worse. We hear about accidents and uneasiness around the world, just so it doesn't hurt
us. We are living safely under God's protecting hand.

I hope these lines will find you in the best of health. I hope
you are able to always be up and take care of yourself. That is a
lot to thank our God for. Your age is beginning to be quite old
and you can expect anything. I will close my letter with Song 92
in Landstad's book. So we will tell each other farewell and wish
God watch over you, etc.

I hope to hear from you some time if we both live for awhile
yet. We don't know when our hourglass runs out.

Be greeted and greet my brothers and their families.

Live well.
Sigri

January 16, 1923

Dear Mother,

Happy New Year in Jesus' name.

> *Time vanishes—the time passes away*
> *It flies hurriedly away, etc.*
> *Yes, so goes daily life.*

Now we are old. We have lived most of our life in this world. This month I will be 67 years old and you, dear mother, are over 80 years old.

I thought these lines would get to you for your birthday, born February 14, 1841. I wish I could drink coffee with you and your old friends. The young people have a word and it is true: We old ones have other interests than the young, so then we gather with the older ones and relive with them old memories in their lonesomeness and forgiveness. Most of the spouses, friends and children have left home, and many of them have gone to their Heavenly home where our time will come soon. Who knows who will be called next this newly begun year. It behooves us to be prepared with oil in our lamps. As it is said, "Be faithful unto death and I will give you a crown of life." Ole Nilsen spoke these words at our Clara's funeral. It is so strange to see the cemetery plot where six of our children are now resting side by side and where we will have our last rest. That will be when our wandering here is broken. God give us a good and blessed farewell time. A verse from a song says, "Sing, pray and listen to what the Lord says. Be friendly and trust. Know that God looks after your welfare. Be wise."

It is a long time since I received your very welcome letter. I send you a very hearty thank you. It was very interesting for us to hear from you and from all known neighbors whom we all have fond memories about. Thousand thanks, also, to your letter writer. I hope he can find the time to write oftener for you but I suppose I'm too demanding.

Here from us and our relatives Knut says everything is well to date. Winter has been nice. We have nice snow so we can use the sleigh. Christmas is over and we had a happy Christmas fest. All our children were home for a week, so we had a good fellowship. At the Christmas tree in church the Sunday School children who helped sing and read were: three from Knut, four from Micheal and three from Cecelia; most of the Sunday school is in the Norwegian language. We are glad for church services from the good old Landstad book. We have used it in the Lutheran Church. There are false prophets who try to snare the believers.

There is no news from here.

Loving greetings to you, dear Mother. A good old age is my heartfelt wish, Mother. Greet my brothers and families as well as other acquaintances who inquire about me and mine. I must not forget the Dengerud girls, Guri and Birgit.

Your Sigri

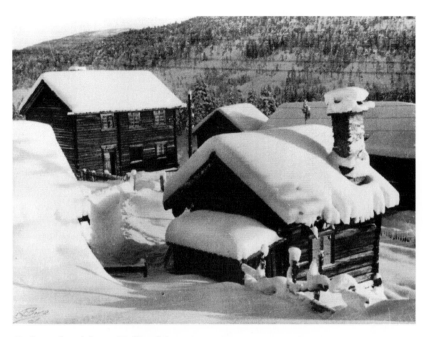

Gudmundsrud farm, Hallingdal, 1945

Gjeldokk farm, Hallingdal, 1945

Nils Knudsen Gudmundsrud

Lars Gjeldaker

Lars Gjeldaker,
Sigrid,
Anna Myking
Gjeldaker

Back: Ola, Nils, and Knut
Front: Lars and Birgit
Gjeldaker

Lars Gjeldaker and
Birgit Myking Gjeldaker

Family in 1891. Back: Anna, Micheal. Middle: Sigrid, Cecelia, Tosten. Front: Clara, Lars

Family in June 1903. Back: Theodore, Anna, Micheal, Cecelia, Clara, Nels. Front: Sigvald, Tosten, Selma, Sigrid, baby Lars

Micheal

"Little" Lars   *Lars*

Sigvald, Clara, Theodore

Clara

Selma at her confirmation

Anna, Cecelia, Clara, Selma

Gathering at Sigrid and Tosten's house

Micheal, Theodore, Nels, Sigvald

Gathering at C. Theo Nelson farm

Clara and
Cecelia

Sigvald, C. Theo Nelson, Cecelia, Store Ole Nilsen

Picnic in the field. Theodore, ?, Sigrid, Sigvald, and Torger

Selma on the threshing machine

Nels and Alfred Bye

Harvest time

Theodore and Tollef

Putting hay in the barn

Sigrid with her sheep

Lars Nelson, Dagny Nilsen, Clara, Selma

Sigrid on skis

*Sigrid at her
spinning wheel*

Anna and Almeda at the Sonsteng home, Anna holding Hardanger

Almeda Sonsteng

Knut Gjeldaker Nelson

Knut Nelson and children. Alice, Clara, Clifford, Beatha, Lionel

Sigrid and Tosten with grandchildren, 1928. Front: Martin Jr., Clara Marie. Back: Edith, Viola, Theresse, Laila, Sylvia, Aleda, Tollef, Almeda, Hilma, Manvel, Arnold, Rudolph

Family in August 1929. Back: Iver, Anna, Micheal, Marie, C. Theo, Cecelia, Sigvald, Hazel. Middle: Sylvia, Aleda, Almeda, Tollef, Manvel, Martin Sr., Selma, Hilma, Laila. Front: Martin Jr., Edith, Theresse, Tosten, Sigrid, Clara Marie, Viola, Ardis, Arnold, Rudolph

Sigrid with grandchildren and great-grandchildren, 1940. Back: Manvel, Tollef, Laila, Almeda, Hilma, Arnold, Theresse, Sylvia, Clara Marie, Edith, Rudolph, Viola. Front: Shirley, Martin Jr., Solveig, Vern, Sigrid holding Helen, Ardis, MeRoy, Michael, Arthur

1942 family gathering

Sigrid in her
Halling bunad

Tosten and Edith on their shared birthday, 1924

Tosten

Sigrid, age 85

Back: Tollef, Sylvia, Lionel. Front: Beatha, Alice, Hilma

Tosten and Sigrid on Tosten's birthday, June 21, 1911

Sigrid and grandchildren in 1940: Laila, Theresse, Sigrid, Almeda

Sigrid and Tosten,
circa 1920

Anna, Sigvald, Selma, Micheal, Cecelia, 1946

Envelope opened by censors during World War I

Letter from September 10, 1894, shows Theodore's "writing" [see page 15 in letters]

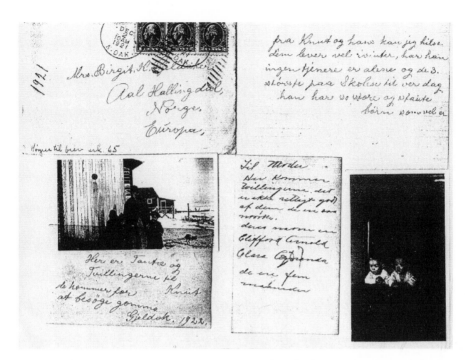

Letters and pictures showing Knut's twins, Clara and Clifford

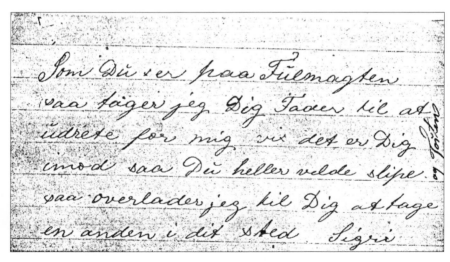

Letter from June 8, 1901 [see page 45 in letters]

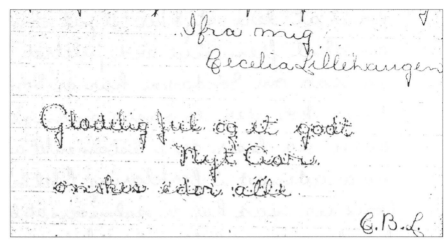

Letter from Cecelia, December 14, 1902 [see page 56 in letters]

Letter from Clara and Anna on left, letter from Cecelia on right, December 14, 1902 [see page 56 in letters]

*March 14, 1896
letter showing
location of Knut's
land* [see page 20
in letters]

Contents page from
Vesterheim

Sigrid's trunk

Organ in log house
[see page 75 in letters]

Sketch of log house by Denise Walser Kolar

Gudmundsrud Family Tree

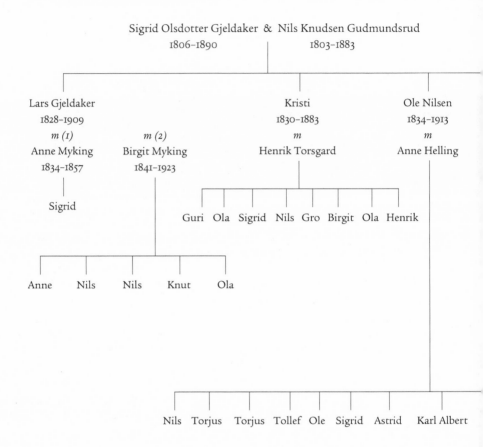

Sigrid Olsdotter Gjeldaker & Nils Knudsen Gudmundsrud
1806–1890   1803–1883

Lars Gjeldaker   Kristi   Ole Nilsen
1828–1909   1830–1883   1834–1913
m (1)   *m (2)*   *m*   *m*
Anne Myking   Birgit Myking   Henrik Torsgard   Anne Helling
1834–1857   1841–1923

Sigrid

Guri Ola Sigrid Nils Gro Birgit Ola Henrik

Anne   Nils   Nils   Knut   Ola

Nils Torjus Torjus Tollef Ole Sigrid Astrid Karl Albert

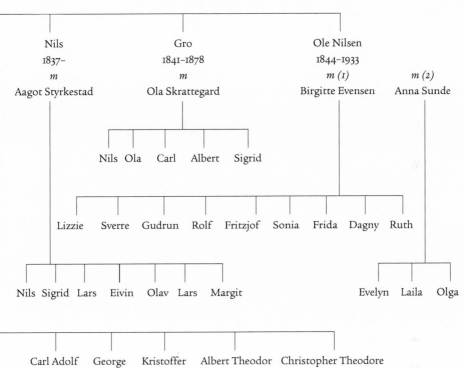

Nils
1837–
m
Aagot Styrkestad

Gro
1841–1878
m
Ola Skrattegard

Ole Nilsen
1844–1933
m (1)
Birgitte Evensen

m (2)
Anna Sunde

Nils Ola Carl Albert Sigrid

Lizzie Sverre Gudrun Rolf Fritzjof Sonia Frida Dagny Ruth

Nils Sigrid Lars Eivin Olav Lars Margit

Evelyn Laila Olga

Carl Adolf George Kristoffer Albert Theodor Christopher Theodore

Lillehaugen Family Tree

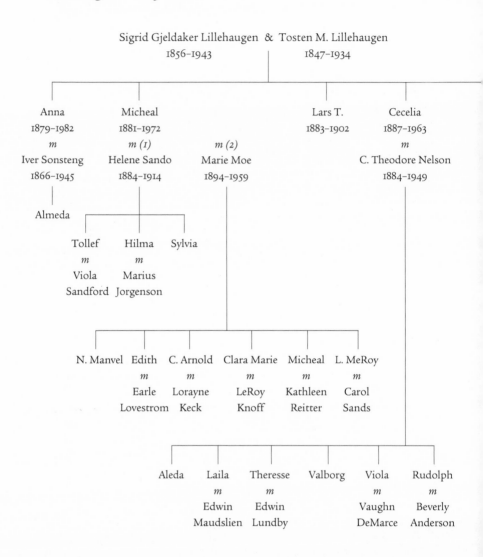

Sigrid Gjeldaker Lillehaugen & Tosten M. Lillehaugen
1856–1943   1847–1934

Anna   Micheal   Lars T.   Cecelia
1879–1982   1881–1972   1883–1902   1887–1963
m   m (1)   m (2)   m
Iver Sonsteng   Helene Sando   Marie Moe   C. Theodore Nelson
1866–1945   1884–1914   1894–1959   1884–1949

Almeda

Tollef   Hilma   Sylvia
m   m
Viola   Marius
Sandford   Jorgenson

N. Manvel   Edith   C. Arnold   Clara Marie   Micheal   L. MeRoy
m   m   m   m   m
Earle   Lorayne   LeRoy   Kathleen   Carol
Lovestrom Keck   Knoff   Reitter   Sands

Aleda   Laila   Theresse   Valborg   Viola   Rudolph
m   m   m   m
Edwin   Edwin   Vaughn   Beverly
Maudslien Lundby   DeMarce   Anderson

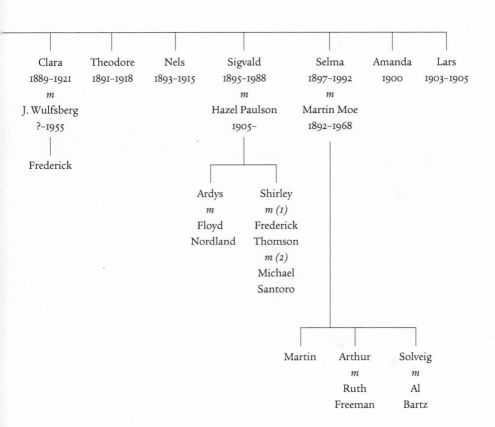

Clara
1889–1921
m
J. Wulfsberg
?–1955

Frederick

Theodore
1891–1918

Nels
1893–1915

Sigvald
1895–1988
m
Hazel Paulson
1905–

Ardys
m
Floyd
Nordland

Shirley
m (1)
Frederick
Thomson
m (2)
Michael
Santoro

Selma
1897–1992
m
Martin Moe
1892–1968

Amanda
1900

Lars
1903–1905

Martin

Arthur
m
Ruth
Freeman

Solveig
m
Al
Bartz

Gjeldaker Family Tree

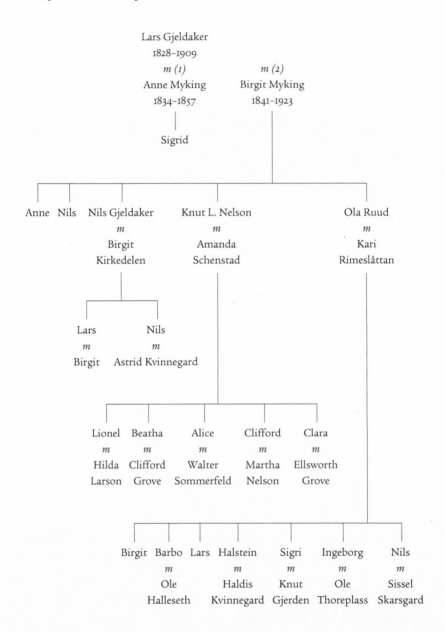

Time Line

1803   Nils Knudsen Gudmundsrud born.

1806   Sigrid Olsdotter Gjeldaker born.

1828   Lars Nilsen Gjeldaker born on April 1.

1834   Anne Myking born.

        Store Ole Nilsen born on June 6.

1837   Nils Nilsen Gudmundsrud born.

1841   Birgit Myking born.

        Gro Gudmundsrud Svendsen (Skrattegard) born.

1844   Ole Nilsen (Rev. Nilsen) born.

1847   Tosten M. Lillehaugen born on June 21.

1856   Sigrid Gjeldaker born on January 29.

1857   Anne Myking died.

1874   Knut Gjeldaker Nelson born on February 13.

1878   Sigrid Gjeldaker married Tosten Lillehaugen on
        April 25.

        Gro Gudmundsrud Svendsen died.

1879   Anna Lillehaugen born on February 14.

1881   Micheal Lillehaugen born on June 4.

1883   Lars Lillehaugen born on August 25.

        Nils Knudsen Gudmundsrud died.

1884   Tosten Lillehaugen emigrated to America.

1885   Sigrid Lillehaugen emigrated to Minnesota with Anna,
        Micheal and Lars.

1887   Cecelia Lillehaugen born on January 12 in Minnesota.

1888   Lillehaugen family moved to Dakota Territory
        (Michigan City).

1889   Clara Lillehaugen born on September 26.

North Dakota became a state.

1890   Sigrid Olsdotter Gjeldaker died.

1891   Theodore Lillehaugen born on November 4.

1892   Knut Gjeldaker Nelson emigrated to Luverne,
        Minnesota.

1893   Nels Lillehaugen born on September 5.

1895   Sigvald Lillehaugen born on August 11.

Knut L. Nelson went to Michigan, North Dakota for
        Christmas.

1896   Nels burned in a prairie fire on October 27.

1897   Selma Lillehaugen born on October 29.

1900   Amanda Lillehaugen born on March 13 and died on
        September 24.

1902   Lars Lillehaugen died on October 28.

1903   "Little" Lars Lillehaugen born on January 8.

1905   Anna Lillehaugen married Iver Sonsteng on August 8.

"Little" Lars Lillehaugen died on October 10.

1907   Micheal Lillehaugen married Helene Sando.

1908   Knut Nelson married Amanda Schenstad on August 28.

1909   Lars Gjeldaker died on September 23.

1910   Cecelia Lillehaugen married C. Theodore Nelson on
        August 1.

1913   *Store* Ole Nilsen died.

1914   Helene Sando Lillehaugen died on July 9.

1915   Nels Lillehaugen died on February 3.

1917   Micheal Lillehaugen married Marie Moe on March 10.

1918   Theodore Lillehaugen died on November 16.

1919   Clara Lillehaugen married J. A. O. Wulfsberg on
        November 11.

1920   Amanda Schenstad Nelson died on February 14.

1921   Clara Lillehaugen Wulfsberg died on March 9.

1923   Birgit Gjeldaker died on April 7.

Selma Lillehaugen married Martin A. Moe in October.

1927   Sigvald Lillehaugen married Hazel Paulson on June 30.

1933   Rev. Ole Nilsen died.

1934   Tosten Lillehaugen died on October 29.

1943   Sigrid Lillehaugen died on March 11.

1961   Knut Nelson died on June 8.

1963   Cecelia Lillehaugen Nelson died on November 16.

1972   Micheal Lillehaugen died on October 24.

1982   Anna Lillehaugen Sonsteng died on August 6.

1988   Sigvald Lillehaugen died on June 30.

1992   Selma Lillehaugen Moe died on June 22.

Names in the Letters

Sigrid often spells individual's names in several ways. For example, she signs her name both "Sigrid" and "Sigri." She calls her brother Knut Nelson both "Knud" and "Knut." She may have used a Norwegian spelling in one letter and an English version in another.

Following is a list of full names mentioned in the letters.

FIRST NAME	LAST NAME
Torger	Aardal
Chr.	Andersen
Pastor Thomas	Anderson
Andrew	Berdal
Lars T.	Bjella
Margit	Bjella
Ole	Bjella (Larson)
Birgit	Dengerud
Guri	Dengerud
Anna	Dok (Dokk)
Helga	Ellingsgaard
Helge	Ellingsgaard
Selvin	Espegaard
Johan (Johanes, John)	Espegaard (Espegard)
Knut	Gjeldager
Lars	Gjeldaker
Sigrid (Sigri)	Gjeldaker Lillehaugen

Lars	Gudmundsrud
Sigri	Gudmundsrud
Sigri	Gudmundsrud Svendsen (Swensen, Svensen)
Mrs. Erik (Turi)	Haakenson
Engebret	Haugen
Asle	Haugo
Botolf	Hefte
Jens	Helland
Anna K.	Helling
Knut	Helling
Lars E.	Helling
Helge	Hoff
Sidsel	Hoff
Borgil	Holto
Aagot	Holtto
Engebret O.	Hougen
Professor E.	Hove
Sven	Huus
Caroline	Jallo
Knud (Knut)	Jallo
Randi	Jallo
Grete	Johan
Birgit T.	Kjeldergaard
Asle	Kortgaarden
Levor	Kortgaarden
H.O.	Kvindegaard
Halvor	Kvindegaarden
Hilda	Larson
Lars	Larson
Amanda	Lillehaugen
Anna	Lillehaugen Sonsteng

Carl Arnold	Lillehaugen
Cecelia (Birgit, Birgita)	Lillehaugen Nelson
Clara Andrea	Lillehaugen Wulfsberg
Edith Theodora	Lillehaugen
Gena	Lillehaugen
Hilma	Lillehaugen
Knut L.	Lillehaugen
Knut S.	Lillehaugen
Lars	Lillehaugen
Lars (little)	Lillehaugen
Micheal	Lillehaugen
Mikkel S.	Lillehaugen
Nels	Lillehaugen
Nels Manvel	Lillehaugen
Selma (Sal)	Lillehaugen
Selma	Lillehaugen Moe
Sigvald K.	Lillehaugen
Sigvald T.	Lillehaugen
Sylvia	Lillehaugen
Theodore	Lillehaugen
Tollef	Lillehaugen
Tosten M.	Lillehaugen
Tosten S.	Lillehaugen
Luella	Lofthus (Johnson)
Margit	Lofthus
Myrtle	Lofthus (Johnson)
Olea	Lofthus (Johnson)
Ronaug	Lofthus
Sander	Lofthus
Turi	Lofthus
Knut O. (Knud)	Loken (Lokken)
Michael K.	Mehus

Marie	Moe Lillehaugen
Nels Nelsen	Mork
Aagot	Myking
Birgit	Myking
Guri	Myking
Knut	Myking
Ole	Myking
Engebret	Mykinghaugen
Knud K.	Nedrebraten
Carl A.	Nelsen (Nelson)
Aleda	Nelson
Beatha	Nelson
C. Theodore	Nelson
Clara	Nelson
Clifford	Nelson
Esther	Nelson
Even	Nelson (Gudmundsrud, Nelsen)
Knut L.	Nelson
Lionel	Nelson
Norris	Nelson
Theresse	Nelson
Valborg Lillian	Nelson
Viola Clarice	Nelson
Bertha	Nestegaard
Knud L.	Nestegaard
Kristi	Nestegaard
Ole	Nestegaard
Svend	Nestegaard
Rev. Ole	Nilsen
(*Store*) Ole	Nilsen (Gudmunsrud, Nelsen)
Sven	Noss
H.C.	Olsen

Aagot	Planting (Bergi)
Asle T.	Rimehaugen
Birgit	Rimeslaaten
Pastor	Ringstad
Ole T.	Rodningen
Syver	Roiseplas
Mabel	Sandelien
Clara	Sando
Helene	Sando Lillehaugen
Jermund O.	Sando
Ole	Sando
Tollef O.	Sando
Amanda	Schenstad Nelson
Gunder J.	Skallehaugen
Kittel	Skallehaugen
Pastor	Skattebol
Alma	Skjervem
Halgrim L.	Skjervem
Lars	Skjervem
Lorin	Skjervem
Mary	Skjervem
Ole	Skjervem
Sadie	Skjervem
Gunhild	Skjervem Lillehaugen, later Larson
L.	Skrefsrud
Aagot	Skrinde
Søndre	Söberseter
Birgit	Sondre
Ole	Sondreal
Sigri	Sondreal
Almeda	Sonsteng
Iver	Sonsteng

Knut	Stave
Levor	Stave
Erik O.	Sundre
Birgit	Svensen
Niels (Nils, Nels)	Svensen (Svendsen, Swenson)
O.	Svenson
Oleiv	Tveito
Ole	Ulshagen
Nels	Vangen
Halvor	Varaberg
Frederick Theodore	Wulfsberg
J.A.O.	Wulfsberg

Gudmundsrud Family

Nils Knudsen Gudmundsrud

Adapted from an article in Hallingdølen

Nils K. Gudmundsrud, "the wisest head in Ål," was a teacher, farmer, and the first local man to serve as Mayor of Ål and Hol. Born in 1803, he had a difficult childhood, living for a time with a farm family at public expense. But he had great potential.

He attended elementary school and received additional teaching from the local pastor. After passing a required examination, he became an elementary school teacher and taught in upper Ål and Kvinnegardslia from 1821-1858. It was said that he was an excellent teacher. Several people remarked, "If it were not for Nils, I wouldn't have learned anything."

In 1833 he bought the Gudmundsrud farm, where he also started a small retail business with Erik Noss (this was the first store in Ål). In 1857 he bought the lower Gjeldokk farm (his wife was Sigrid Olsdatter Gjeldokk). In 1868 he sold the Gudmundsrud farm to their son Nils. In 1869 he sold the Gjeldokk farm to their son Lars, who took the name Gjeldaker.

Gudmundsrud was smart, temperate, and considerate. He was an excellent writer and had fine handwriting. People in the area asked him to write letters, legal papers, probates, etc. He was also handy at making implements for the farm, including a row seeder made from wood. (This machine is in the Bygd museum in Ål.)

Gudmundsrud was much respected as a civic leader. He served as the first local mayor of Ål from 1844-1849, and again from 1856-63. He was also the first director of the Ål Sparebank, from 1870-71.

Lars Gjeldaker

Like his father, Nils Knudsen Gudmundsrud, Lars Gjeldaker was a renowned teacher. When he was 12 years old, he served as a substitute teacher for his father. This meant that when he went to confirmation, some of his classmates were also his students in the school.

Gjeldaker became a teacher when he was 19 and taught for 51 years, from 1846 to 1897. In 1878 he obtained a degree from the Teacher's school in Voss, following which he received a pay increase according to his years of experience.

In his day, he was considered the finest teacher in Ål. He faced many challenges as a teacher, but was known for always being kind, loving, and gentle with children. He had a unique way of motivating children so they wanted to learn. He had a lively imagination and was a master storyteller. He was most exceptional when he taught Bible history, Norway's history, and Catechism.

The biggest fear for a teacher was when the bishop or the supervisory pastor came to visit. Then the teacher had to present the confirmation class in the church and question them on their lessons for approximately 15 minutes. However, Gjeldaker did not become nervous. Indeed, when Dean Faerden visited, Gjeldaker continued to question the children for an additional half hour.

In 1896 he resigned from teaching. School officials presented him with the King's Medal for his fine work as a citizen. Over one hundred people attended this special festival; ninety were former pupils. After his retirement, he served as a substitute teacher for two years, even though he was 68 years old.

Like his father, Gjeldaker was well known for his writing skills. People still commented about his handwriting years later.

Gjeldaker was a deeply religious man. He took part in a religious movement in the 1850s and conducted numerous home Bible studies. Many people came to him with their deepest spiritual questions. He wrote a history about the pastors in Ål, and helped build a new church.

In civic affairs he was involved in politics, and helped start the Ål bank. He also did family research and wrote his memoirs.

Ole Nilsen

Ole Nilsen emigrated from Hallingdal in 1866. He first went to Estherville, Iowa, to be near his sister, Gro Gudmundsrud Svendsen. Later he went to Luverne, Minnesota. After the death of his wife and four of his adult sons in 1895, *Store* Ole journeyed to Norway with his daughter Sigrid and son Carl. Sigrid remained in Norway, marrying Hartvig Stangebye, and their descendants live in Oslo. Carl returned to Minnesota and lived in Minneapolis. Nilsen lived in retirement at Northwood, ND, at Bemidji, MN, and died in Scandinavia, WI. His youngest son was C. Theodore Nelson, who married Cecelia Lillehaugen.

Gro Svendsen (Swenson)

Gro Gudmundsrud Svendsen became known for the letters she wrote to her parents after she went to America with her husband, Ole Skrattegaard (also known as Svendsen or Swenson). They settled in Iowa. Her letters were preserved and made into a book called *Frontier Mother*.

Reverend Ole Nilsen

Reverend Ole Nilsen was a prolific writer of books, stories, articles, poetry, and hymns. He emigrated from Norway in 1871 and attended Augsburg Seminary in 1873. He started his ministry in Iowa in 1874. In 1892 he and his family moved to Scandinavia, Wisconsin, where in addition to his ministry, he served as Chairman of the Board of Directors of the Scandinavia Academy for 27 years. In 1920 he retired in Grand Forks, North Dakota. In retirement, he edited *Hallingen* from 1922-1933.

Gudmundsrud Family Publications

Lillehaugen Family Treasures
by Theresse Nelson Lundby

Family Treasures contains Tosten Lillehaugen's autobiography and Sigrid Lillehaugen's firsthand account of her journey from Hallingdal to Minnesota. It also includes writings and photos of the extended family of Tosten and Sigrid. Copies are available from Theresse Lundby, Greenbush, MN 56726.

Store Ole Nilsen Gudmundsrud
by Theresse Nelson Lundby

Ole Nilsen Gudsmundsrud (*Store* Ole) wrote several letters to family members in Norway during the years 1866-1880. This collection includes the account of his journey from Norway to America in the 1860s and several photos. The original letters reside at the Minnesota Historical Society in St. Paul, MN. Copies of the book are available from Theresse Lundby, Greenbush, MN 56726.

Frontier Mother: The Letters of Gro Svendsen
Translated and edited by Pauline Farseth and Theodore Blegen.

Gro Gudmundsrud Svendsen wrote to family members in Hallingdal, Norway, from 1861 to 1877. In her letters she describes her pioneer life in Iowa. The book was published in 1950 by the Norwegian American Historical Association. The book is out of print, but is available on microfilm. Contact the NAHA in Northfield, MN 55057.

Luther's Life
by Rev. Ole Nilsen

An account of Martin Luther's life, published in 1917 by Augsburg Publishing House.

Dalrosen
by Rev. Ole Nilsen

"Rose of the Valley," published in 1928 by Augsburg Publishing House.

Memories and Impressions
by Nels Manvel Lillehaugen

This collection includes Manvel's stories about his life, including his military experiences during World War II. It also includes poignant stories about the shortened lives of Nels Lillehaugen and Theodore Lillehaugen, sons of Sigrid and Tosten Lillehaugen. The book is out of print.

Papa's Letters
by Beatha Nelson Grove

"Papa" refers to Knut Nelson Gjeldaker, son of Lars Gjeldaker and half-brother of Sigrid Lillehaugen. These letters were obtained from the archives in Ål, Norway, and translated by Beatha Nelson Grove, Knut's daughter. For a copy of the book, contact Beatha Grove, Adams, ND 58210.

Letters of Longing
by Frida R. Nilsen

A collection of letters by Pastor Ole Nilsen and his wife, Evelyn Birgitte Evensen, written while Ole was in America and Evelyn was in Norway. Frida Nilsen, their daughter, translated and published the letters. The book is out of print.

Growing Up in the Old Parsonage
by Frida R. Nilsen

Description of Frida's childhood experiences in the parsonage at Scandinavia, WI. The book is available from Olga Berglund, 910 Cannon Valley Drive, Northfield, MN 55057.

What Became of Little Ole?
by Olga Nilsen Berglund

Story of the life of Pastor Ole Nilsen Gudmundsrud (Little Ole), written by his youngest daughter, Olga Berglund. Several photos included. The book is available from Olga Berglund, 910 Cannon Valley Drive, Northfield, MN 55057.

Notes on the Authors

Theresse Nelson Lundby is the daughter of Cecelia Lillehaugen Nelson (daughter of Sigrid and Tosten Lillehaugen) and Christopher Theodore (C.T.) Nelson (son of *Store* Ole Nilsen Gudmundsrud and Anne Helling).

Nels Manvel Lillehaugen (known as Manvel) was the son of Micheal Lillehaugen (son of Sigrid and Tosten Lillehaugen) and Marie Moe.

Beatha Nelson Grove is the daughter of Knut Nelson and Amanda Schenstad Nelson, and the niece of Sigrid Lillehaugen.

Frida R. Nilsen was the daughter of Reverend Ole Nilsen and Evelyn Birgitte Evensen.

Olga Nilsen Berglund is the daughter of Reverend Ole Nilsen and Anna Sunde.

Historical Notes

Carding Wool

Carding is a process by which wool fibers are opened, cleaned and straightened in preparation for spinning. Sigrid's cards were two flat pieces of wood covered with thin metal teeth. The two cards were moved back and forth, up and down, one card in each hand, to comb the piece of wool.

Sigrid states in a letter that she had worn out her set of cards and needed another set. Very likely these would be sent from Hallingdal with the next emigrant coming to the area, or with a Halling-American who was visiting Norway.

Sigrid spoke often of her flock of sheep. They were her joy. She sheared the sheep each spring and prepared the wool. Her grandchildren recall her sitting at the spinning wheel, either singing or telling the little ones about her childhood in Norway. She was happy—her blue eyes sparkled as she worked and reminisced. She used the yarn to knit mittens and stockings for grandchildren, for missions, and for others in the area.

Church Strife

The early settlers organized congregations shortly after their arrival in America. Meetings were held whenever a pastor was able to come. People first met in homes, later in schoolhouses, and finally in churches. Pastors lived twenty or more miles away. In the early years, they traveled by oxen and horses. When the roads improved, they could use automobiles.

The strife mentioned in the letters refers to the fact that the community was divided into two groups of Norwegian Lutherans, one associated with the United Church and the other with the Synod Church. Although these two groups united in 1917, the two congregations (whose churches were four miles apart) continued to be served by different pastors. In 1944 the two congregations merged, and in 1949 they moved their two church buildings to Whitman and joined them into one structure. This structure still stands, and the congregation still meets regularly.

Cook Car

The cook car was a covered wooden structure on wheels that held a coal burning stove, a washbasin, utensils, food, and a table. The cooks were usually young women in their late teens.

Threshing time meant long days for the cooks. A typical day began at 4:30, when they would light the lamps and stoves and begin cooking. They carried water for drinking, washing, and cooking from a well in the farmyard. Then the cooking started: breakfast, mid-morning lunch, noon dinner, mid-afternoon lunch, and supper. Each hearty meal was cooked entirely from scratch. In addition, they baked eight or more loaves of bread each day, along with cakes, cookies, and pies.

Distances from the Lillehaugen Farm

Whitman	4 miles
Pelto	7 miles
Brocket	10 miles

Michigan	13 miles
Petersburg	19 miles
Fordville	20 miles
Lakota	20 miles

English School and Norwegian School

English school was another name for the public school. Many of the newcomers attended school in order to learn the English language.

Norwegian school was designed to teach children the Norwegian language and provide religious instruction. This served as a prelude to confirmation instruction by the pastor.

Gudmundsrud and Gjeldaker

In Norway, families took the name of their farms as their surnames. Gudmundsrud was the name of the farm that Nils Knudsen Gudmundsrud purchased in 1833 and sold to his son Nils in 1868. Gjeldaker (or Gjeldokk) is the name of the farm that Nils K. Gudmundsrud bought in 1857 and sold to his son, Lars Gjeldaker, in 1869.

Post Office

Prior to the establishment of Rural Free Delivery, it was necessary to establish country post offices. On April 1, 1898, Tosten Lillehaugen became the postmaster of the Sarnia post office, which was in his home. At first the mail came three days a week, from Lakota via Pelto to Sarnia. In 1904 the mail came daily from Brocket. Even though Rural Free Delivery was established on November 1, 1906, the Sarnia post office continued to operate, as several people lived too far away from the route. In 1914 the Sarnia post office was discontinued.

Country post offices served as community centers and played an important part in the lives of early pioneers. The Sarnia post office was a melting pot for three nationalities: the Bohemians to the north, the Finns to the west, and the Scandinavians to the south and east. Most of them did not speak English, so they would sit in their huddles, each speaking their native language, making quite a conglomeration of sounds.

The postmaster in those days received no salary or commission on stamps sold, and there were no money orders in such remote areas. The only income was cancelled stamps. Letters required two-cent stamps, so 50 letters had to be mailed in order to earn one dollar. Registration of letters helped, as it required an eight-cent stamp to register a letter. In that case, it took only ten letters to earn a dollar (two-cent stamp plus eight-cent registration).

Railroad and Grain Shipments

In 1910–1911 the Soo Line came to the area, and towns such as Whitman were built along the line. The ability to ship grain from the farmer's elevator in Whitman was a big improvement. Now the farmers in the area could haul grain four miles instead of thirteen (as they previously did to Michigan). Distances mattered, as horses were the only means of transportation for many years.

Roads and Snow Roads

Over the years, road surfaces progressed from dirt roads to gravel to black top. Better roads, better automobiles, and snow removal changed life in the rural areas.

"Snow roads" were a unique feature on the prairie. After the first snowfall, farmers changed the wheels on their hayracks and wagons to sleigh runners. Then the traveling was done either on regular roads or on shortcuts across open fields. After considerable use, the snow road became packed and snow usually drifted past it during storms. In the spring, the snow roads melted last.

Rural Electricity

In 1935, President Franklin D. Roosevelt established the Rural Electric Administration. In 1938, a Rural Electric Cooperative was organized in Whitman. One of the first generators in the area was located at the C. Theodore Nelson farm, where Cecelia Lillehaugen Nelson lived. Prior to the REA, farmers who wanted electric lights used 32-volt storage batteries to supply the electricity.

Sarnia

Sarnia was named after a city in Ontario, Canada. Sarnia Township was in northern Nelson County, less than a mile from the Lillehaugen farm. The post office at the Lillehaugen home was called Sarnia, even though it was located in Walsh County. Sarnia was also the name of the congregation in Whitman, Sarnia Lutheran Church.

Telephone Service

The telephone came to the area in 1909. Farmers bought two shares at $50 each in order to build the line from Michigan. This was a "party line" with many subscribers on one line. Each farm had a different ring, such as one long ring, two short rings, one long ring.